The Truth
About God

Stanley M.
HAUERWAS
William H.
WILLIMON

The Truth About God

THE TEN COMMANDMENTS
IN CHRISTIAN LIFE

Abingdon Press
Nashville

THE TRUTH ABOUT GOD
THE TEN COMMANDMENTS IN CHRISTIAN LIFE

Copyright © 1999 by Abingdon Press

This book is printed on acid-free paper.

Library of Congress Cataloging-in-Publication Data

Hauerwas, Stanley, 1940-
   The truth about God : the Ten commandments in Christian life / Stanley M. Hauerwas, William H. Willimon.
      p.   cm.
   Includes bibliographical references and index.
   ISBN 0-687-08202-1 (alk. paper)
   1. Ten commandments.   I. Willimon, William H.   II. Title.
BV4655.H345   1999
241.5′2—dc21   99-18398
                                                                            CIP

Scripture quotations unless otherwise noted are from the New Revised Standard Version of the Bible. Copyright © 1989 by the Division of Christian Education of the National Council of the Churches of Christ in the United States of America. All rights reserved.

Scripture quotations marked RSV are from the Revised Standard Version of the Bible, copyright © 1946, 1952, 1971 by the Division of Christian Education of the National Council of the Churches of Christ in the USA. Used by permission.

Quotations from *John Calvin's Sermons on the Ten Commandments* by John Calvin, translated by Benjamin Farley. Copyright © 1980. Used by permission of Baker Book House Company.

Selections reprinted from THE LARGE CATECHISM OF MARTIN LUTHER, copyright © 1959 Fortress Press. Used by permission of Augsburg Fortress.

01 02 03 04 05 06 07 08—10 9 8 7 6 5 4

MANUFACTURED IN THE UNITED STATES OF AMERICA

To
Sarah Freedman
and
Jacqueline Andrews

*Hear, O Israel: The L*ORD *is our God, the L*ORD *alone. You shall love the L*ORD *your God with all your heart, and with all your soul, and with all your might. Keep these words that I am commanding you today in your heart. Recite them to your children and talk about them when you are at home and when you are away, when you lie down and when you rise. Bind them as a sign on your hand, fix them as an emblem on your forehead, and write them on the doorposts of your house and on your gates. . . . When your children ask you in time to come, "What is the meaning of the decrees and the statutes and the ordinances that the L*ORD *our God has commanded you?" then you shall say to your children, "We were Pharaoh's slaves in Egypt, but the L*ORD *brought us out of Egypt with a mighty hand. . . . He brought us out from there in order to bring us in, to give us the land that he promised. . . . Then the L*ORD *commanded us to observe all these statutes, to fear the L*ORD *our God, for our lasting good, so as to keep us alive."*

— Deuteronomy 6:4-9, 20-24

Contents

Preface

We hope that *The Truth About God*, a conversation on the Ten Commandments, will be read by those who read our book *Lord, Teach Us*. That book, on the Lord's Prayer, exemplifies what we most care about. For we seek nothing less than to help us recover how the most basic Christian practices can and do offer us the salvation wrought in Christ.

In this book we try to exhibit why our confession that God has claimed us through Jesus' cross and resurrection cannot be an isolated "belief" abstracted from the practices of a people who have learned to speak truthfully to one another. And we believe speaking truthfully is a necessary skill if we are to be a people capable of surviving as resident aliens.

We continue to be sustained by those who make us more than we are. We are particularly blessed by spouses who often tell us the truth even when we do not wish to hear it. For Patsy and Paula we thank God. Alex Sider and Jason Byassee read the manuscript and spared us from many mistakes. Sarah Freedman and Jackie Andrews not only typed and retyped this manuscript but literally do the work that makes our work possible. Therefore, it gives us great pleasure to dedicate this book to them.

> *Anyone who knows the Ten Commandments perfectly knows the entire Scriptures.*
>
> —Martin Luther, *The Large Catechism*

A People Owned by the True God

A large claim to be sure, even for Luther. Yet we believe it is true. Everything depends on what one means by "know." You are reading this book because you want to know about the Ten Commandments. By the end of the book we hope to convince you that *knowing* the commandments requires a lifetime embodiment of a set of practices peculiar to the church—practices as basic as confessing belief in the Father, Son, and Holy Spirit. To understand how such a confession is tied to not stealing is what it means to know these commandments "perfectly."

Furthermore, we believe that recovery of the commandments is crucial for our survival as a people called Christian in the face of today's challenges. One of the curious challenges we face is from those who think they know the commandments.

A judge in Alabama fights to have the Ten Commandments on the wall of his courtroom in order to say that the law enacted in his court is based upon the law of God. Yet, we believe, in a U.S. courtroom the commandments so displayed are not the Ten Commandments of the God whom Christians worship as Father, Son, and Holy Spirit.

Others defend the commandments as a means of calling America back to basic morality, a universally valid code of conduct, absolutes upon which all people of goodwill can agree. Because the commandments come from the one true God who made heaven and earth, they are "universal," but not in the sense many count as universal.

While we can understand, in the face of this morally chaotic society, actions such as putting the commandments in a courtroom, we hope to show that they are a misuse of the commandments. A few years ago, newsman Ted Koppel gave what was to be the most popular commencement address at Duke University in recent decades. After enumerating various signs of moral decay in America, Koppel asked, "What is the solution for all these problems?" He then proceeded to list each of the Ten Commandments, briefly explaining how, if Americans would only follow these ethical guidelines, we would have no moral problems.

We agree that if Americans would adhere to the Ten Commandments this would be a better place to live, though we disagree with Koppel's implied characterization that the Ten Commandments are timeless ethical principles that are applicable to all Americans. We shall see that the first thing to be discovered in the commandments is not that we are potentially righteous but that we are presently sinners.

We cannot understand the commandments, the Decalogue ("Ten Words"), apart from the worship of the true God. Those who do not worship that God will catch a glimpse of that God when they, for example, tell the truth. But the obeying of an isolated commandment is not to know the commandment "perfectly." The Ten Commandments are meant for those who are known by the God of Abraham, Isaac, Jacob, the God of Jesus Christ. The commandments are the way we learn to worship the true God truthfully, not the way we make American democratic pluralism work.

Recall the context. Israel is in slavery in Egypt. Before Moses, a murderer minding his own business in Midian, a bush bursts into flame. There is a voice:

I have observed the misery of my people who are in Egypt; I have heard their cry on account of their taskmasters. Indeed, I know their sufferings, and I have come down to deliver them from the Egyptians, and to bring them up out of that land to a good and broad land.

—Exodus 3:7-8

Here is no Deistic "Unmoved Mover" of a God. Here is a God who hears, intrudes, acts, cares, calls. God says to Moses, "I am going to deliver my people and guess who is going to help me." Moses protests; God insists. Moses is told to go to Pharaoh and tell this most powerful man on earth to let the Hebrews go. Why? Because God is against slavery? No. God demands freedom from Egyptian slavery so that the Hebrews may go out into the wilderness to worship (Exodus 3:18).

Pharaoh of the "hard heart" resists. There are negotiations, confrontations, frogs, plagues, gnats, and much death. Finally Pharaoh relents, saying, "Go, worship the LORD. . . . Be gone" (Exodus 12:31-32). Israel hastens toward the desert. There, at last they are liberated, free!

Well, not quite. The Hebrews have been liberated from slavery in order to worship in the wilderness. But it has been so long since anyone has worshiped the true God, they have forgotten how. Is the liturgy of the God of Israel high church or low? Should incense be used? What about vestments? Moses is summoned to the top of Mount Sinai (Exodus 19:20). There the Lord opens the conversation by reminding Moses of what has been done for Israel, thus indicating who God is:

I am the LORD your God, who brought you out of the land of Egypt, out of the house of slavery; you shall have no other gods before me.

—Exodus 20:2-3

Tell the Israelites: You have seen what I did to the Egyptians, and how I bore you on eagles' wings and brought you to myself. Now therefore, if you obey my voice and keep my covenant, you shall be my treasured possession out of all the peoples. Indeed, the whole earth is mine, but you shall be for me a priestly kingdom and a holy nation.

—Exodus 19:3-6

This is a not-so-gentle way of reminding Israel, "I paid dearly for you. You have been brought out of slavery, not in order to be free from all attachments, but rather in order that you might more fully belong to me, that you might worship me."

How are they to worship? Here begins the enumeration of the commandments. "Don't have idols." "Don't steal." "Don't have sex with other people's spouses." Moses surely thinks, *This doesn't sound like any service I've ever attended.*

Surprise. This God has a peculiar notion of worship in comparison with other gods. Some gods are into war or sex or gold. Here is a God who wants a holy people, a family where everyone is clergy.

The important word here is *therefore.* Because a people has been saved by God, therefore this people is to be a nation of priests. When Exodus says that Israel is to be a "holy nation," it means a people set apart, "resident aliens" as we have said elsewhere.[1] When it says "priests," it means that Israel exists for the sake of the whole world, to intercede, to make sacrifice, and to mediate—to live in such a way, in obedience to the commandments, that other less enlightened and obedient peoples will say to themselves, "Surely this great nation is a wise and understanding people" (Deuteronomy 4:6 RSV).

Thus evangelism has its basis in the joyful obedience and worship of the true God by a people who, despite ourselves, are being made truthful by our worship. The Ten Commandments are made for all people, but the way we discover that is by seeing their embodiment in the people of Israel. In particular such a people is necessary if we are to understand why the commandments require one another, why no one commandment can stand on its own.

This is the very same language picked up by the First Epistle of Peter when it claims that, by the grace of God, even we Gentiles have been subsumed into Israel's vocation to be priests to the world in the name of the God of Israel and Jesus:

But you are a chosen race, a royal priesthood, a holy nation, God's own people, that you may declare the wonderful deeds of him who called you out of darkness into his marvelous light.

—1 Peter 2:9 RSV

The Ten Commandments must be read and lived within the background of this vocation given by a saving God. Christians live as those who have been chosen by God, called, claimed, possessed, owned by God that we might proclaim, in word and deed, what God has done. We live by the commandments as a way of worshiping the true God. When we thus worship the true God, we show forth to the world the sort of people God is able to produce. Our little lives are caught up in the great purposes of God for the world. We become commandeered for purposes beyond ourselves. We, for whom lying, deceit, and falsehood come quite naturally, are transformed by our obedience into a people of the truth.

The rabbis (*Mekhilda de-Rabbi Ishamael*) asked why, if the Ten Commandments are so important, God waited so long on the Exodus to give them to Israel. The rabbis answered, "Suppose a man entered a city and said, 'I shall rule over you.' The inhabitants would say, 'Who are you and what have you done for us?' What did the man do? He built a city wall, aqueducts, led them in battles. Then he declared, 'I shall rule over you,' and they gladly said, 'Yes!' "

Similarly, God brought Israel out of Egypt, divided the Red Sea, provided food, then, late in the Exodus, God said, "I shall rule over you" and Israel answered, "Yes indeed."[2]

We, who were slaves, have become free. But that does not mean that we are free from all attachment, free to "do our own thing." As one of the Jewish prayers puts it, "We were freed from being slaves to Pharaoh so that we might become slaves to Torah."

The commandments are not guidelines for humanity in general. They are a countercultural way of life for those who know who they are and whose they are. Their function is not to keep American culture running smoothly, but rather to produce a people who are, in our daily lives, a sign, a signal, a witness that God has not left the world to its own devices. We have the Decalogue because we have been delivered and redeemed by God. We are delivered and redeemed by God because we have the Decalogue. These "Ten Words" both constitute Israel and the church and critique us in our common life. So this book about the Ten Commandments intends to be both a gracious reminder of who we are and an abrasive prod to be who we ought to be.

Are we hereby saying that one must believe in God in order to be moral? The question implies that we already know what is "moral" and who is "God." Christians are not primarily people who "believe" something religious, but rather we are people who have been called to live the sort of lives in community whereby if this God does not exist, the way we live our lives makes no sense. "Belief" is too flaccid. When Christians are busy believing, we are not assenting to a set of religious platitudes, we are putting our bodies on the line, betting every day that God rules the world, that God's way will triumph in the world. Thus Luther could say that to "know" the commandments is to know everything that Scripture is about.

Morality and God

By the end of this book we hope that you will agree that Christians mean something quite different from what the rest of the world means by "morality" and "God." Of course, even people who do not know God can be "moral." We have a friend who is a perfect pagan who would never steal or cheat or kill. As Christians we must be taught to see our friend's morality arising not from some abstraction called "morality," but because he is also a creature of a good God, a creature who was created to desire to serve and to worship that God. So, in a sense, the Decalogue is a kind of "natural law" that mirrors who we are created to be. But we can only discover that law through transformed witnesses who embody the whole law. That is why what our friend means by "lying" may not be what we mean. But at least we have somewhere to begin conversation.

When we do talk together about morality, we will find how characteristic it is for Christians to begin by speaking first about the church, by what it means to worship God. Apart from this community, the commands of God appear heroic, impossible, idealistic, or just odd. Church, a community of the forgiven, a people who keep coming together to worship God, makes the commandments intelligible. In fact we might put on the Decalogue a warning: *Don't try to obey any of these commandments alone.*

The commandments are our distinctive way of doing politics—the formation of a truthful community (i.e., church). Of course, this is the way God would have all creatures live, so we believe that life in the commandments is evangelistic. It is our privilege as Christians to exemplify a life that is possible for all and, if in our living of the commandments our neighbors are attracted to Christ on the basis of our lives so formed, so much the better.

But before the Ten Commandments are about us, they are about God. We know one another through speech—speech that is often wordless. We know the true and living God because this God has refused to stay aloof, unconcerned, and taciturn. Our God could have stayed on Mount Sinai, hidden in the clouds, silent. Instead, the true God called Moses and had him write down what would please God. Our relentlessly self-revealing, loquacious God has spoken "Ten Words" to us and is thereby known to us. Before the words, and behind each of them, is a God, the sort of God who tolerates no rivals like Pharaoh or the Pentagon, a God who does not leave us alone to stumble aimlessly in the wilderness or in Winetka but graciously gives us the law "for our good always, that [God] might preserve us alive" (Deuteronomy 6:24, RSV). The sort of God who would give us the commandments is also the God who would give us Jesus.

Furthermore, the commandments signal to us that this thing between us and God matters. God desires us and enlists our aid in reclaiming a lost creation. Salvation of the world turns on our obedience, on how we have sex and handle property and watch our words. Although it is clear that we are addressed as community, a nation, a people, in the plural, each of the commandments is put to us in the second person singular: *You.* A claim is made on each of us. This God does not speak to us just through a professional priestly caste. This God speaks to each of us in simple, direct words we can understand, addressing each of us where we live, where there are real issues about property and sex and speech. Here is a God who loves us like wives and husbands love each other in marriage. God gets jealous for us. The relationship between us and God is not one of abstract, high-flown principles and ideas. It is a relationship between a God who loves and a people who are loved enough to be told how, when, and where to return that love. As one of our Jewish friends says, "Any God who won't tell you what to do with your pots and pans and genitals isn't worth worshiping." The sort of God who would give us the commandments is also the God who would give us a Savior born of a virgin.

The Ten Commandments are an affirmation that, thank God, God has not done everything that needs doing in this world but has left plenty for us to do as obedient and faithful people. God, having been creative, faithful, and just, now gives us the means to act the same. What God wants done graciously includes us. God uses us to bring life out of death, order out of chaos, light into the darkness. Whenever we are obedient, it is called *worship.* Where we work Monday through Friday becomes an altar, and we get to be the world's priests. As Jesus told his people, "You did not choose me but I chose you. And I appointed you to go and bear fruit" (John 15:16).

The commandments were given to Israel after liberation from slavery, right after Israel had entered the wilderness, as a gift to the redeemed. However, that they were given these directives was also a sign that Israel was still being redeemed, was still on the way. Exodus keeps on happening among the obedient and the faithful. God keeps coming to us in the commandments and we keep coming to God. The commandments are terse, concise, with not much detail. That means there is much room for us to ponder and to argue about their application, lots of space for us to keep growing in what it means to be faithful, room still left for yet another book like this one!

The commandments sound platitudinous. Most everyone agrees that one should not commit adultery (all right, *almost* everyone agrees). But what do we mean by "adultery" as Christians in a society that practices marriage as serial monogamy, a world where Ronald Reagan, who was praised as a moral exemplar, lived with his second wife in the White House? We don't tend to call that "adultery," but Jesus did (Matthew 19:1-12).

We hear the commandments say that we should not steal, and we think we agree. But before we can agree on stealing, we must have some notion of what is "ours." The Marxist claim that capitalism is a form of stealing probably comes close to the biblical idea of "ours." In Israel, the refusal to share the gleanings of the fields with the poor would have been understood as a form of thievery. Thus Jesus was forever saying, "You have heard it said, but I say . . ."

So to "know the commandments," by which Luther claimed one can know the whole Scripture, means that these commands are not self-interpreting. They depend on the practices of a community (church) formed by the worship, in Spirit and in truth, of a trinitarian God. We don't know what adultery is apart from a church that shows us what marriage is. We don't know what the commandments condemn as stealing apart from a church that rearranges our concept of "ours." So obedience and knowledge of the commandments begin in the Sunday worship of the church, by focusing not on the commandments, but first on the God who says, "I am the Lord your God, who brought you out of Egypt, out of the land of slavery."

All authority in heaven and on earth has been given to me. Go therefore and make disciples of all nations, baptizing them in the name of the Father and of the Son and of the Holy Spirit, and teaching them to obey everything that I have commanded you. And remember, I am with you always.

—Matthew 28:18-20

The commandments are therefore a means of living in a world out of our control. Placing the commandments on the wall of a U.S. courtroom implies that somehow these commandments can be abstracted from the worship of God and is a clear violation of the third commandment. As a result the commandments are at best reduced to a truncated "natural law," or worse, some innate code of morality that usually focuses on the so-called second table of the Decalogue as if those commands make sense abstracted from the first. The Protestant Reformers taught that a major function of these commandments is revelation. In attempting to obey the commandments, we learn the extent of our sinfulness and the means of our redemption. Thus the commandments name a way of life made possible only by our initiation (baptism) into a community where there are regular opportunities for confession, forgiveness, and reconciliation. Again, we cannot obey the commands of the Decalogue on our own. We could not stand the force of Jesus' "obey everything that I have commanded you" if it were not for his "I am with you always."

That the commandments are so straightforward and terse suggests not that they are easy to know, but that they are not self-sufficient, fixed rules for life in general. No one should feel smug, secure, or complacent in the commandments, because not everything that God wants to say to us in every occasion in life is said within them. That they are terse is a means of driving us toward God and God's people, realizing that we can be good only as a gift of God's continuing revelation. There is still more to be said in the conversation between us and the Trinity, and there is always a chance that we can get it wrong. Humility is thus not only a by-product of the worship of the true God, but also an expected aspect of our attempts to be faithful to the truth that is God. The commandments are a chief means by which our lives are bent toward the way and will of God. This is not a bad definition of worship in Spirit and in truth—*bending life toward God.*

Stanley M. Hauerwas and William H. Willimon
Duke University
Pentecost, 1998

Notes

1. Stanley M. Hauerwas and William H. Willimon, *Resident Aliens: Life in the Christian Colony* (Nashville: Abingdon Press, 1989) and *Where Resident Aliens Live* (Nashville: Abingdon Press, 1996).
2. Roger Brooks, *The Spirit of the Ten Commandments* (San Francisco: Harper and Row, 1990), 63.

Chapter One

> *You shall have no other gods before me. You shall not make for yourself an idol, whether in the form of anything that is in heaven above, or that is on the earth beneath, or that is in the water under the earth. You shall not bow down to them or worship them; for I the LORD your God am a jealous God, punishing children for the iniquity of parents, to the third and the fourth generation of those who reject me, but showing steadfast love to the thousandth generation of those who love me and keep my commandments.* *
>
> —Exodus 20:3-6

The First Commandment

Our story begins with the voice of God. God is the initiator of this "conversation." If God had not loved enough to speak, there would be no conversation, no Israel, no nation of priests, no story called "church," no us. Unlike the laws found in Deuteronomy or elsewhere in Exodus, the commandments are in

---

*We have made a decision to follow Lutheran and Catholic practice, which makes "You shall have no other gods before me" and "You shall not make for yourself an idol" the first commandment. The Jews and the Reformed (the followers of Calvin) make "I am the Lord your God who brought you out of the land of Egypt" the first commandment and "You shall have no other Gods before me" the second. A friend has suggested that when the Reformed tradition embraced the practice of making the prohibition against idols the second commandment, as part of their polemic against images in the medieval church, they ended up making God

the form of direct address from God, thus underscoring their force. God speaks to Israel the way parents sometimes speak to children—directly, pointedly, without equivocation or much qualification. Do not steal. Do not kill.

Furthermore, everything rests upon, "I am the LORD *your* God." Command arises from relationship. Israel is owned, called, and therefore accountable. Anything that is demanded of Israel rests upon God's election and gifts to Israel, one of those gifts being the Law.

In few places in Israel's testimony about God is it more evident that our assumed distinction between ethics and theology is simply unknown than in the light of this commandment. Freedom from slavery to the empire first requires an active, holy God, a God whose holiness stands against every rival claim to sanctity. So the first commands assert the uniqueness, the oddness of the God who has loved Israel. The true God, who stands at some distance from Israel, is to be obeyed and worshiped, not used or recruited in behalf of our purposes—even when those purposes are called "ethics."

Israel's God commands. Walter Brueggemann calls command the "defining and characteristic marking" of the true God.[1] The most striking characteristic of communication between God and Israel is that of command-obedience. Because we live in a culture where submission to any authority other than our own egos is considered unduly authoritarian and unfair, command-obedience is difficult for us. We have freed ourselves from all external authority except servitude to the self. This we hail as freedom, though Israel testifies that slavery (particularly slavery as the necessity to do "what I want to do") comes in many guises.

Sometimes slavery comes from Pharaoh, who ordered, "Go and get straw yourselves, wherever you can find it; but your work will not be lessened in the least" (Exodus 5:11).

Sometimes slavery comes from an economy that says, "Buy a lot of Pepsi, get a lot of stuff."

So the issue is not *if* we shall live under some external command,

---

so inexpressibly distant that Deism was the inevitable result. As we note in this chapter, Deism is a big problem for modern people, so if we can help defeat Deism by a numbering of the commandments, so much the better.

but rather *which* external command will have its way with us. Israel knew the burden of imperial, governmentally sanctioned command. The Exodus was not the achievement of unrestricted, boundless freedom, for such freedom, as we have said, is a modern fiction. The Exodus was not liberation. It was about an exchange of masters, the false for the true.

We were created to be God's good lovers, but everywhere we find we have been enslaved by our choices. That we are so enslaved has everything to do, as we will see in our discussion of the last commandments, with desiring rightly. Part of the problem is our current presumption that freedom is *choice* rather than *desire.* God created us as passionate beings. We rightly desire. The problem is when our desire becomes disordered by desiring what is desirable as if God does not exist. The result is slavery.

For they are my servants, whom I brought out of the land of Egypt; they shall not be sold as slaves are sold.

—Leviticus 25:42

Just to the degree Israel is closely tied and utterly obedient to the commandments of the true God, and therefore animated by well-ordered desire, Israel is truly free. God knows that Israel, left to its own devices in the wilderness, is prone to reestablish Pharaoh's rule in different forms. So the commandments are given as a basis for a radically alternative society that is counter to all that the empire demands. There can be no resistance to the empire, no ongoing alternative without a counter institution. The commandments are the basis for this alternative way of life for Israel.

The first commandment is odd to lay upon modern people. It is irrelevant, some say, because modern people have outgrown the propensity to worship a plethora of gods—polytheism— rather than one God. Our modern problem is, they say, whether or not we should have any God at all—atheism. The trouble is, atheism is not a biblical issue. The Bible never asks, "Is there a God?" Rather, the Bible question is, "*Who* is the God who is there?"

Even atheism is parasitic upon a notion of God. We believe that the great problem of the modern age is not atheism. Our problem is the kind of limp, flaccid rejection of God so characteristic of late-twentieth century Europeans and their colonies. Seldom these days is atheism the angry shaking of the fist against some alleged injustice of God. More than likely, atheism is little more than the shrug of the shoulders that says something like, "I don't care what someone believes about God as long as he is sincere," or "It doesn't matter so much what someone believes as long as that person lives a good life."

That shrug of the shoulders, that simpleminded agnosticism is the result of Christians disobeying the first commandment, attempting to reduce God to a problem of belief rather than a call to worship. We are those who are not to have any other gods (and the commandment appears to assume that there are indeed many). Listen to us pray and one might get the impression that we think we are doing God a favor by believing in God. The commandment is clear: God does not want our "belief." God wants all of us, heart, soul, pots and pans, the whole ball of wax:

Hear, O Israel: The LORD is our God, the LORD alone. You shall love the LORD your God with all your heart, and with all your soul, and with all your might.

—Deuteronomy 6:4-5

Luther put the matter this way:

What is it to have a God? What is God? The answer: a God is that to which we look for all good and in which we find refuge in every time of need. To have a God is nothing else than to trust and

believe him with our whole heart. As I have often said, the trust
and faith of the heart alone make both God and an idol. If your
faith and trust are right, then your God is the true God. On the
other hand, if your trust is false and wrong, then you have not the
true God. For these two belong together, faith and God. That to
which your heart clings and entrusts itself is, I say, really your god.
The purpose of this commandment, therefore, is to require true
faith and cling to him alone. The meaning is: "See to it that you let
me alone be your God and never seek another." In other confidence of the heart, and these fly straight to the one true God and
words: "Whatever good thing you lack, look to me for it and seek
it from me, and whenever you suffer misfortune and distress, come
and cling to me. I am the one who will satisfy you and help you
out of every need. Only let your heart cling to no one else." *(The
Large Catechism,* 9)

Luther's God is no Deist. The first commandment is not about
a God whom we construct out of our belief that something had
to start the world moving, but whatever that something was is no
longer capable of much action. The first commandment is about
being addressed from outside our frames of reference, about
being commanded by a God who is jealous. God's jealousy has
everything to do with being a saving God. The jealousy of God
can be understood as the logical attitude of the God who brought
us out of the land of Egypt, out of the house of bondage.

Christians know this God as the same God who raised Jesus
from the dead. Just as God delivered Israel from bondage in
Egypt, we know this miraculous God as God of the Resurrection.
Robert Jenson reminds us that God is jealous because our God is
a God who is fully invested in time. Other gods not so invested
care little about their identities because they have no stake in
time. But our Lord is a jealous God who would be known by temporal events of Exodus and Resurrection. The worship of other
gods may be enabled by identifying names and descriptions, but
these are transcended in the name of still greater mysteries in
which it is assumed the very boundaries of time are broken. Not
so the God of Scripture. Our Lord is a passionate, timely Lord
who can be found in Cross and Resurrection.[2]

That God is the God of Abraham, Isaac, and Jacob is the way

God makes time. That is, by making covenant and partnership with Israel in order to redeem the world, God gives the people a story. This God jealously wants to be known as the One who yoked himself with a people. Christians, when we believe we shall have no other gods before us than the Trinity, believe not that we are superior to the Jews, but that we worship the same God who jealously demanded Israel's love in the first commandment. When we say "Trinity" or "Father, Son, and Holy Spirit," it is our compressed, shorthand way of telling the whole story of redemption as narrated in all of Scripture, that is, the God who called Abraham out of Ur is the same God who raised Jesus from the dead.

That our God is so known, so worshiped, has everything to do with why Luther could say that to know the Decalogue is to know all of the Bible. The commandments are storied in the sense that, to understand them properly, we must know the great overarching story—Creation, Exodus, kingship, prophets, exile, Jesus, death, Resurrection, Ascension, church. The commandments also *story* us, that is, they help subsume us into the story we call redemption. It is also true to say that the commandments make such a story possible. That is why, as we shall see, the commandments are necessarily interrelated—or, put differently, why all the commandments are constituted by the first commandment.

The first commandment is central to the life of Israel and that of the church. Here we are reminded that our God is not beyond this world, this life, this time, but enmeshed in time, making possible that which would otherwise be impossible. Any god who was above time would not do us much good. Calling God "jealous" is a biblical way of noting God's passionate involvement with us.

The God of Israel has a personality that is characterized by deep self-regard. The Hebrew word for "jealousy" denotes intense emotional reaction to any affront to God's sovereignty and glory. Moreover, the emotion stressed here is overbearing and white hot. As Walter Brueggemann says, this God is no "cool administrator of an ordered realm, but is engaged with strong feelings about all that is due Yahweh which is in every case."[3] There can be no rival to this God. Because this God is so intensely, emotionally connected to Israel, any disobedience on the part of Israel evokes harsh and intense emotional response for God.

You cannot serve the LORD, for he is a holy God. He is a jealous God;
he will not forgive your transgressions or your sins. If you forsake
the LORD and serve foreign gods, then he will turn and do you harm,
and consume you, after having done you good.

—Joshua 24:19-20

Time and again, Israel ventures a conversation with this God, hoping for a cool, detached consideration of Israel's situation. Immediately, Yahweh heats up the rhetoric. Angry words are exchanged. Israel, which hoped only to be chided for some small transgression, is called "adulterer," "fornicator." Conversations between Israel and God quickly become heated, emotional, loud, conflicted. God's relation with Israel often has the same heatedness that characterizes marital arguments, rhetorical flourish better suited to a bedroom or a kitchen than to a carpeted sanctuary full of good church people.

The words from the true God tend to be heated because much is at stake. God has risked much to deliver and to choose Israel, risked death and the cross to make church. Therefore, matters between us and God are rarely small or inconsequential. This God has a passionate, particular commitment to Israel and the church and expects passionate obedience in return.

The LORD goes forth like a soldier,
like a warrior he stirs up his fury;
he cries out, he shouts aloud,
he shows himself mighty against his foes.

—Isaiah 42:13

God is engaged. Israel and the church forever attempt to tame and to domesticate God. It can be a fearful thing to be in conversation with a God who deals with such extremes of love and anger, anger that arises out of God's love for righteousness. There is some anxiety occasioned by our attempts in worship to be in conversation with a God who is free, just, and sovereign, a God who will not be enlisted, even by those whom God loves. Time and again, in submission to this God, we are reminded of the great gap between our kingdoms and the kingdom of God. There is huge space between us. And yet, one of the most beloved aspects of Israel and the church is the bold intimacy of a people who dare to converse with a living God. There is, in Brueggemann's words, in this claim that God is jealous, a "largeness and roughness . . . a power and intensity. . . . This is a God who will be taken seriously, who will be honored and obeyed, who will not be mocked. The nations are warned; and Israel is also on notice. Yahweh must be taken in full capacity as sovereign; there is no alternative."[4]

Something in us would like a calm, cool, and detached Deistic deity. We wish sometimes that our God could be a cool and dispassionate administrator, just applying and enforcing the rules, the great bureaucratic American president in the sky who is fair to everyone without distinction. But the true God is much more involved in creation than that. This God is jealous, like an angry, possessive husband (Ezekiel 16:38), and yet a loving one. This God, unlike us, cares so much about justice that God is capable of righteous indignation. This God, on occasion, even weeps (John 11:35).

Christians claim that this self-involved emotional attachment, this intrusive presence of God, finds its culmination in the Incarnation. For us, the Old Testament ends with God deeply concerned, filled with pathos for Israel. In the Incarnation, in the advent of the Christ, God's intense self-involvement moves toward enfleshment in Jesus. God becomes extravagantly, personally, fully engaged with God's people. Thus, the radical engagement of God as Incarnation in the New Testament is definitely prefigured by the radical engagement of God with God's people in the Old Testament. This God will have a family, even if the price is quite high. The detached god of the philosophers is countered by the God who tends to go overboard in determination and passion for his people. At times, that passion is Israel and the church's great gain, at times it is our great burden. It takes a great people to be loved by so great and living a God!

After a wholesale rejection and condemnation of Israel, Hosea hears God speak as a yearning husband,

Therefore, I will now allure her,
and bring her into the wilderness,
and speak tenderly to her.

       —Hosea 2:14

We would not know this pushy, passionate God if God had not first addressed us, saying, "I am the Lord your God who . . ." Against the ideas of Ludwig Andreas Feuerbach, this God is not our wishful projection of human needs, our egos inflated and called "God." If we were projecting a god, surely we could have projected a more compliant, congenial one than Trinity!

This God is not a projection of our needs, but rather the One who saves by transforming our need. Israel came out into the wilderness assuming that bread was its most basic necessity. On Sinai God told Israel that even more than bread it needed vocation. Jesus demonstrated his oneness with God when he began his ministry in the wilderness, when, having been offered bread by Satan, he told Satan what Israel learned through the commandments:

It is written,
"One does not live by bread alone,
but by every word that comes from the mouth of God."

       —Matthew 4:4

The existence of Israel and the church is concrete, visible testimony to the world that it is possible for people's desires to be formed not by the way the world gathers people—race, class, gender—but on the basis of nothing but the word of God. Every Sunday when we gather, it is not our huddling together in the hope of fulfilling our collective narcissistic desire, but rather we convene in the conviction that our life together is based upon the call of God or else we are nothing.

Again, Jenson says, "According to the claim that the God of Israel makes for himself, Israel did not envision her God by the needs of her culture, but rather *He* chose Israel, *with* her culture."[5] Such a God calls into question all accounts of religion that would make satisfaction of some generalized, projected human need the same as believing in God. Later in the commandments, when this God commands unusual things of us like having sex only with one person (in violation of our basic instincts for survival) we shall have concrete evidence that God is not something we thought up.

The First Commandment in Christian Life

The Jews have continued to teach Christians that we don't need God—*we worship God.* That is the first commandment, to stop attempting to get something out of God and instead to bend our lives toward God. It is only in worship, in this constant, repetitious (it must be habitual, weekly, because it is so against our sinful inclination), bending of our lives toward God, that we are freed from the idolatries that constantly threaten. It is only in worship of God that we learn how complex and serious our inclination is toward idolatry.

Idolatry is more than simply giving homage to finite realities, as destructive as that may be. Idolatry consists in the denial of the true God through failure to trust the only One who may be trusted. Idolatry is the assumption that salvation can come elsewhere than from the God who commands, *You shall have no other gods before me.*

When we say Father, Son, and Holy Spirit, Christians believe we are still talking about the one God who made heaven and earth and who sustains it still. We are not talking about three gods, for God is "jealous," zealously cherishing God's unity. That God is Father we know through the Son who is creator and redeemer. That God is Son we know by the Father who raised Jesus from the dead. That God is Holy Spirit we know through the bread and wine made Christ's body and blood. That God is Trinity is the Christian reminder that our story, our community, is unintelligible without the story of Israel and the people called Jews. There is no God but this God. There are no other gods each with its peculiar sphere of influence. We do not believe as Christians that the world is divided into competing, warring camps, each with its own divine patron. Against such division and warring chaos, Israel taught us to proclaim, "The LORD your God is one . . ."

Idolatry is also the ever-present danger of thinking that it might be possible for us to effect our own redemption by our obedience, our enlightenment. God's world is so good and God has endowed humanity with such gifts that we can be tempted to believe that we are sufficient unto ourselves. Deism is this form of idolatry. It is the conceit that the Creator has left us creatures fairly much on our own, that Christ has no hands but our hands, that it is up to us to do right or right will not be done, that we have, living as we do in a democracy, the responsibility to make the world turn out right. The devastating results of Deism are all around us as we end what may be the bloodiest century the world has ever known.

Prayer is the protest against idolatry. In prayer, we give the Creator what is due, acknowledging the joyful surprise that we exist. Moreover, in prayer, we claim our existence as gift, grace. The Decalogue is God's gift to Israel continually to teach Israel how to live, not by wits, but through gift.

John Wesley noted that the first commandments concern our duty to God. "It was fit those should be put first, because man had a Maker to love before he had a neighbor to love, and justice and charity are then only acceptable to God when they flow from the principles of piety" (*Explanatory Notes on the Old Testament,* Exodus 20:2).

But we do not believe that the first three commandments ought to be separated from the others. It is only in loving God that we know how to love the neighbor without destroying our neighbors. We can truly love our neighbor as a creation of God and we can only know our neighbor as creature when we know our Creator.

The quest for autonomy (literally, self-law), for independence, self-sufficiency, to have ourselves as gods unto ourselves, is often seen as the hallmark of modernity. Faced with the apparent meaninglessness of a world without God, we assume that a major modern task is to create or impose meaning. In contrast, the Decalogue reminds us that the meaning of our lives is given through the discovery that we are indeed creatures of a gracious God who gives us all the time in the world to live in trust with one another. Meaning is a by-product of having been addressed by God in the first commandment.

Furthermore, modernity did not succeed in killing the gods, but rather it succeeded in fostering rampant superstition. Modern people like to think that as we become more educated, liberal, enlightened, the less we need to worship gods. No. We appear to have been created to worship, and worship something we will. Thus we superstitiously construe our lives as in the grip of the Fates. Luck becomes our secular theology. Life becomes one great casino (there is some sort of link between the recent rise of lotteries and other forms of legalized gambling and modern superstition). "When your number's up, it's up," we say. Rabbi Kushner's popular book *When Bad Things Happen to Good People* says that God is mostly uninvolved in the good or bad that happens to us. Life is a big roulette wheel and what can anybody do? Prometheus, Eros, Mars, Psyche, the list of deities appears to be exploding, as human activity is inflated to the level of the divine. Toward the end of this century, having bankrupted the Russians, we exchanged worship of the almighty Bomb for veneration of our genitals (a cult with a long and noble tradition). Affluent Western people, having satisfied so many of life's basic needs like food, housing, and clothing, now beseech the gods not for bread, but for mutual orgasm.

We wonder if modern superstition is due not only to our breaking of the first commandment, but also to a misunderstanding of its prohibition against images. God is transcendent, but it is a transcendence known through God's nearness. God is Trinity, which means that God is incarnate in Jesus of Nazareth, making possible our ability to see God.

Thus the church defended the veneration of icons, not only of Christ but also of Mary, the Mother of God, of angels and saints, because we know God incarnate. Seeing God's self-giving in Jesus, sacramentally encountered at the Lord's Table and in baptism, we are given the means to resist temptations to idolatry.

Our God is not ineffable. Bill Phipps, moderator of the United Church of Canada, probably thinks he is being intellectually humble in saying, "I don't believe that Jesus was God, but I'm no theologian. . . . The whole concept of the nature of God is broader and wider and more mysterious and more holy than could be expressed in Jesus."[6] Arrogance is another way to characterize the desire for a God "broader and wider and more mysterious," the arrogant unwillingness to worship God who comes to us in the form of a Jew.

For instance, a Harvard theologian complains that the God of Israel and the church is far too "exclusive" to be helpful in ameliorating contemporary religious differences, which she considers to be at the heart of most contemporary political conflict.[7] That anyone could blame contemporary conflict upon either God or gods, rather than upon the murderous nation states, is surprising to us. Who is the "god" she would have us worship? "God is our way of speaking of a Reality that cannot be encompassed by any one religious tradition, including our own."[8] In other words, our experiences of the divine make God, rather than God producing our experiences. So we begin by worshiping tolerance, or pluralism, or some other secular virtue as a way to deal with a violent world, then attempt to salvage those aspects from the Jewish and Christian Scriptures that conform to our predetermination of what the world needs before it knows God.

Again, one of the great gifts of the Ten Commandments for people like us, people who would rather have a broad-minded Deist God than the one we have in Jesus, is the irreducible specificity of the commandments. Eschewing broad concepts like "pluralism," the commandments stick to no-nonsense, straightforward speech and basic, concrete demands. Christianity, arising out of Judaism, rather than say, Hinduism, has the great virtue of simplicity. There is little that is esoteric, ineffable, obscure, and mystical. All we have to do is to worship, in all that we do or say, the

God who is Father, Son, and Holy Spirit who has first addressed us.

Note that in this commandment God promises punishment for those who disobey the first commandment, those who get confused in worship. Why does God have the need to be so exclusive? Why get so worked up over a bit of idolatry among friends? It is not that we will be punished for our sin, but rather our sin itself is punishment in that it is painful not to be who we were created to be. False gods can be so demanding. Monogamy tends to take less work and far less rationalization than adultery. And, as Bob Dylan says, everybody serves somebody.

Millard Fuller spoke on the Duke campus, telling about how he and his wife prayerfully decided to sell everything they had, leave a successful law practice, move to a poor neighborhood in Americus, Georgia, and wait for God to tell them what to do next. Eventually, God told them to start building houses for poor people, and thus Habitat for Humanity was born.

Later that week, one of us was asked, "How old were Fuller's children when he and his wife pulled up and moved to Americus?"

We were slow to get the point of the question until it was asked more than once. Behind the question was the modern sentimentality: It's fine for you to have some religious experience if you want, but it's not fine for you to drag your children into it with you, to ask them to sacrifice for your values.

The person who asked the question has a sixteen-year-old daughter on birth control pills and a son who has been hospitalized for alcohol abuse.

The first commandment reveals to us the sobering truth that all of us are sacrificing our children to some god or another, that all of us parents routinely ask our children to suffer because of our values, and well we should. Our idolatry is, as the first commandment says, passed on as punishment to our children. Thus the 1552 *Book of Common Prayer* specified that the commandments were to be read every Sunday before the Confession of Sin to signify that we know ourselves as sinners only because the commandments reveal our true selves to us.

The good news, the gospel, of the first commandment is that

God has done an extraordinary thing—God has given us his name.[9] God has entrusted to us the means whereby we might faithfully worship the true God. If we fail, we also fail our children. Punishment is not a sign that God is weak, having to extract obedience only through threat of punishment. Punishment is the facts of life in lives lived without God. We are not punished for sin, but sin is punishment. The ability to see is a gift whereby God reaches out to us to show us the way back home. When we cry out in the dark, in our lostness, the One who answers is the One who longs to have us come home, the One in whose worship is home.

Notes

1. Walter Brueggemann, *Theology of the Old Testament* (Minneapolis: Fortress Press, 1997), 182.
2. Robert Jensen, *Systematic Theology* (New York: Oxford University Press, 1997), 47.
3. *Theology of the Old Testament,* 293.
4. Ibid., 295.
5. *Systematic Theology,* 52.
6. As quoted in *The Christian Century,* December 17, 1997, 1185.
7. Diana Eck, *Bozeman to Bararas* (Boston: Beacon Press, 1993).
8. Ibid., 169.
9. Eck (pp. 170-78) ridicules the notion that God has a name and that name has been spoken to us, arguing that such anthropomorphism leads to arrogant exclusivism. We hear her refusal to consider that God's name might just be Trinity as, we hope, the last gasp of modernity's arrogant refusal to believe that God just might have chosen Israel to tell the world the name above every other name.

Chapter Two

> *You shall not make wrongful use of the name of the LORD your God, for the LORD will not acquit anyone who misuses his name.*
> —Exodus 20:7

The Second Commandment

We meet a stranger and ask, "What is your name?" To name ourselves to another is a move from estrangement toward friendship.

Romeo asks, "What's in a name?" adding "A rose by any other name would smell as sweet."

Romeo is wrong. Names are more than arbitrary labels. To tell a stranger your name can be among the most intimate of human exchanges. There is power in a name, power in being able to call someone by name. In Genesis, humanity is shown to have "dominion" when God gives humanity the power to name the animals (Genesis 2:19-20).

Blessed be the name of the LORD
from this time on and forevermore.
From the rising of the sun to its setting
the name of the LORD is to be praised,
The LORD is high above all nations.
—Psalm 113:2-4

Christians, as adopted members of the house of Israel, are privileged to be among those to whom God's name has been given. The second commandment arises out of that gift. This command makes clear why any attempt to separate theology (talk about God) from ethics (obedience to God), or any severance of worship (the service of God) from morality (the service of God) is wrong.

But Moses said to God, "If I come to the Israelites and say to them, 'The God of your ancestors has sent me to you,' and they ask me, 'What is his name?' what shall I say to them?" God said to Moses, "I AM WHO I AM." He said further, "Thus you shall say to the Israelites, 'I AM has sent me to you.'"

—Exodus 3:13-14

To know God's name, to have received this great gift from God, requires that we rightly use the name. The most "religious" act we perform is prayer, for it is done "in Jesus' name." Jesus even promised that where only a couple of us are gathered in his name, he would be there in the midst of us (Matthew 18:20).

To be able to call God's name entails moral obligation. Because we had to be told God's name, we cannot make God mean anything we want. God must reveal who "I AM" is through loving actions toward Israel and by the resurrection of Christ. Revelation is the way we name our discovery that God has discovered us. God has chosen to come close to us, to be intimate, to reveal the "name that is above every name" (Philippians 2:9) in order that we might joyfully witness to the whole world that we have not been left to our own devices. We joyfully witness that we have been given the means whereby we can get to God because God, in revealing God's name, has gotten to us. We are to fashion lives that demonstrate the power of knowing how to address God by God's proper name,

. . . so that at the name of Jesus
every knee should bend,
in heaven and on earth and under the earth,
and every tongue should confess
that Jesus Christ is Lord,
to the glory of God the Father.
— Philippians 2:10-11

The trouble is, we seem lately to have forgotten that for us "God" is not an experience we have had but rather a proper name we have been given. We have become confused into thinking when we hear "God" that we are hearing a description of some vague, allegedly universal human experience ("Everybody believes in God, even those who do not believe in Jesus") rather than a name. "God" is the name Christians are told to call Trinity—Father, Son, and Holy Spirit. You cannot get this name through long walks in the woods, hugging trees, delving into your psyche, sitting quietly in your room, or getting in touch with your inner child. This God cannot be known other than by revelation. Any other claimant to the name "God" is an idol and the first commandment has already warned us about idolatry.

"Look, the virgin shall conceive and bear a son,
and they shall name him Emmanuel,"
which means, "God is with us."
— Matthew 1:23

A recent Bible study group had as its task the study of the book of Leviticus. One of the group members, a young gay man, began the group's discussion by noting, "Because of my sexual orientation, I have always feared reading this book of the Bible. We all know that Leviticus is against gays. Right? Well, to my surprise,

Leviticus is against a lot of things! I found rules in here for how to cook, how to eat, how to treat farm animals. The amazing thing to me is how concerned God is about so many little, every-day, domestic problems! What kind of God would care about how we have sex, even more about how we make dinner!"

It was a wonderful realization of the peculiarity of *this* God who is not ashamed to be called our God.

Because our ethics begin in a meeting with this God and in our vocation to worship the Trinity, rather than in our attempts to be ethical, we don't think much of those who make a strict distinction between law and gospel. We are particularly distrustful of those who use the Pauline contrast between law and gospel to distinguish between Judaism and Christianity. We don't believe that Jesus has come to preserve us from the bondage of Jewish "legalism" in order to enable us to have Christian "freedom."

It is a libel against the Jews to accuse them of "legalism" when they obey the commandments in their love of Torah. For Israel, the Law is gospel, the good news that God has graciously revealed himself and his way to us through the Law. Christians differ from Jews, not because Christians are opposed to "law," but rather because we believe that Christ fulfills the promises of God in the Torah. Saint Paul objected to life by the Law because he had become convinced that Christ was all that Torah demanded. True, Christians read the Ten Commandments differently from Jews, but not in the way that is assumed by the traditional contrast of "law" with "gospel." You know how this is popularly presented: The Jews have a religion of judgment, whereas we have a religion of grace. The Jews stress law, whereas we stress love. This is a bad characterization of the commandments.

Israel has taught us that nothing can make us happier than obedience to the law of God for in this law is our life. Obeying the law is to be who God has created us to be and in that being is our true happiness. Nothing can make us any more free in a capitalist, consumer-driven society than to find something true enough to free us from our bondage to ourselves. To be attached to the law of God and thereby to be free from ourselves is good news.

The law of the LORD is perfect,
   reviving the soul;
the decrees of the LORD are sure,
   making wise the simple;
the precepts of the LORD are right,
   rejoicing the heart;
the commandment of the LORD is clear,
   enlightening the eyes; . . .
More to be desired are they than gold,
   even much fine gold;
sweeter also than honey.
          —Psalm 19:7-8, 10

The Christian good news, the gospel, is the claim that complete obedience to God is found in the life, teaching, death, and resurrection of Jesus of Nazareth and in the continuing work of his Spirit. We believe that the second commandment refers to Jesus, so that when we pray "in Jesus' name," we believe that we are praying in the name of God. In the third commandment we believe that the Sabbath has been taken up and renewed by Jesus" resurrection, changing the way that time is understood. So now our sabbatical, our day of rest, is made possible by the resurrection of Jesus in which God's intention for Creation has been restored in Jesus.

Similarly, the first commandment's prohibition against images has been, for Christians, reconfigured through God incarnate in Jesus. Therefore Christians do not forbid all images, because God incarnate effected a new economy of how the created order witnesses to the One who rightly commands our worship. While there are great overlaps in the way Christians and Jews interpret the commandments, a different narrative—Bethlehem, Golgotha, the empty tomb—shapes our reading.

That narrative determines that we must get out of our heads the notion that the commandments are a short list of do's and don'ts, rules to be obeyed. The commandments are first about the kind of people we ought to be and the sort of deeds one might expect from people who are formed on the basis of the story of Jesus. The commandments keep reminding us that ethics are not so much, "What ought I to do?" but rather, "Who ought I to be now that God has invaded the world as Jesus?" Questions about "What to do?" are only intelligible against the background of that story.

No strict distinction ought to be made between our being and doing. It is a two-way street. Sometimes in keeping the commandments, we become better people than we could have been if we had named ourselves. At other times, the power for our obedience to the commandments is derived solely from the affection for God engendered in us by naming God in our worship. So not taking the Lord's name in vain begins by saying the Creed, by being reminded that we fear and love the One who has first loved us by graciously, and at some risk, giving his name to us. In confessing our faith by reciting the Creed we say both who we are and perform an action that embodies who we are.

Not taking the Lord's name in vain means that we are committed to speaking truthfully to God, to ourselves, and to one another. Our prayers ought to be honest.

My Father, if it is possible, let this cup pass from me; yet not what I want but what you want.

—Matthew 26:39

We ought to keep practicing telling the truth to God and to one another:

O holy and merciful God,
   we confess that we have not always taken upon ourselves the yoke
   of obedience,
      nor been willing to seek and to do your perfect will.
We have not loved you

with all our heart and mind and soul and strength,
neither have we loved our neighbors as ourselves.
You have called to us in the need of our sisters and brothers,
and we have passed unheeding on our way.
(Prayer of Confession, *The United Methodist Book of Worship,* 1992,
474)

Luther observed in his *Large Catechism* that "to lie and assert under his name something that is not so" is to take God's name in vain (p. 17). Not only are Christians to live truthfully but we must also speak truthfully. So much of the time we speak as if God did not matter, as if nothing decisive has transpired between us in having been given God's name. Our speech to God and neighbor becomes loose. We flatter, we say too much. The prophets of God long ago complained of those false prophets, those flatterers who tell people what their "itching ears" (2 Timothy 4:3) want to hear, crying "peace" when there is no peace (Jeremiah 6:14). Paul condemned those lying preachers whose talk was lovely, but without substance. "Word merchants," Paul called them. With so much loose talk about God, some of the prophets predicted a time when there would be a "famine of the word" (Amos 8), when God, so sick of our insincere speech, grows silent.

Sometimes we wonder if today's church and its speakers have so little to say because we are being punished for having taken the Lord's name in vain. Little wonder that God has little to say to those who have not practiced custody of the tongue.

Never be rash with your mouth, nor let your heart be quick to utter a word before God, for God is in heaven, and you upon earth; therefore let your words be few.

—Ecclesiastes 5:2

Most of us thought it odd that Khomeini called a Salman Rushdie novel "blasphemous." It is not for us to decide on Islamic grounds whether Khomeini was right or wrong to do so. Yet most reactions to Khomeini's edict indicated that many American Christians no longer believe blasphemy to be a problem, a thought that is itself blasphemous. Blasphemy is speech that makes God part of our lies. And it is a sign of our infidelity that we are no longer outraged by it. As Aquinas observed, when we swear by God it is nothing less than to call God as witness, and thus when we swear falsely we indicate to our neighbors that God loves lies (which, according to Psalm 5:6, God hates).

Blasphemy is not only when a National Endowment for the Arts subsidizes an artist who drops a crucifix in a jar of urine, but also when German soldiers marched off to World War II bearing *"Gott mit Uns"* ("God with Us") on their uniforms. That was blasphemy, taking the Lord's name in vain, attempting to drag God's good name through the mud of our sin. Not much less blasphemous was George Bush asking for a prayer in our behalf before we bombed Iraq.

The Second Commandment in Christian Life

Because of our deceitful speech, church too often becomes not a place of truth telling, but a conspiracy of niceness where we flatter people, telling them what we think they want to hear rather than the truth, in the hope that they will treat us the same. A friend of ours who took the cure with Alcoholics Anonymous says he can't go back to church because, having experienced the searing honesty of his A.A. group, church seems like a superficial gathering of flatterers.

"I'm not all that well off, after all."

"Ten percent after taxes is as much as we can afford to give."

"My work is so demanding I simply do not have time for Bible study."

"Abortion was the only alternative I had."

"I may not be the best person in the world, but at least I am not a hypocrite."

"This church believes in racial inclusiveness."

In a wonderful sermon on the second commandment, Calvin says that we ought to speak reverently, not just of God, but also of all God's works, even the weather:

When speaking of the weather, whether it is fair or rainy, we are nonetheless confronted by the marks of God's majesty. When he sends us bad weather he reveals himself as a judge to make us aware of his anger [in order] that we might examine our sins, grieve, and be led to repentance. If, instead of being humbled before God and displeased with having offended him, we are provoked, as we commonly see others filled with contempt, is it not fitting that this weather should last a long time? And so we do not flee back to our God; we do not ask him to forgive our sins. And such is the case in everything else. (*Sermons on the Ten Commandments*, 94)

That we regard Calvin as having gone "a bit too far" in asking us to stop complaining about the weather is but indication of how difficult it has become for us to conceive of our lives as wholly determined by God's life. Having told ourselves that we are creators rather than creatures, we live as if there were no Creator. The curse, "God damn you," is a vain use of God's name just to the extent that it implies that God will damn according to our wishes. In such cases, our "ethics" become another means of attempting to live our lives independently, autonomously, as if there were no God or as if we were gods unto ourselves.

That God promises to punish those who abuse his name is good news, for it tells us that we matter to God's life. To us has been given the cherished name that is above every other name. We therefore know not to refer to ourselves as "heterosexual" or "American" or "self-made," but rather as those who have been baptized and have thereby had the name of Jesus laid upon us. Even as God has trusted us enough to tell us the truth about ourselves in the cross of Jesus, revealing the lie behind our vaunted self-esteem, so in the church we can trust our sisters and brothers to be people who are able to hear the truth from one another without hating one another for being truthful. Most people will tell you that they lie to other people because they are so nice—they don't want to hurt anyone. Self-concern, rather than true concern for others, is behind most of our lying, but we like to think of ourselves as nice people who put the feelings of others before telling the truth. So doctors routinely lie to patients, and patients lie to doctors, and preachers say too much or too little to their congregations, and the congregations praise their preachers for their flattering sermons, and we become people characterized more by our deceit than our discipleship.

When we published *Resident Aliens,* we received a number of letters from people outraged that we had the nerve to use the story of Ananias and Sapphira in Acts 5 as if it were still relevant to our lives. We like the story, not only because it reports on an interesting church meeting (when so many church meetings are so dull) but because God got so mad at two of the most prominent members of First Church that both of them were struck dead during the meeting and had to be carried out and buried before adjournment!

Interestingly, when Peter confronts Ananias and Sapphira, he does not accuse them of greed or materialism, but of lying. Furthermore, Peter does not accuse them only of lying to the leaders of the church, but of lying to God (Acts 5:5). That's quite a claim. To lie to the church is to lie to God. No wonder the story ends with, "And great fear seized the whole church" (Acts 5:11)!

In most of today's church, we don't believe in killing people for lying. We are willing to sacrifice the Body of Christ in order to keep things pleasant. Our point in our treatment of this wonderful scriptural text in *Resident Aliens* is that it is invigorating, in this story, to be in the presence of a church that believes that being a truthful community under the name of God is a matter of life and death.

When you heard the second commandment, perhaps you immediately thought of that portion in the Sermon on the Mount where Jesus says,

Again, you have heard that it was said to those of ancient times, "You shall not swear falsely, but carry out the vows you have made to the Lord." But I say to you, Do not swear at all, either by heaven, for it is the throne of God, or by the earth, for it is his footstool, or by Jerusalem, for it is the city of the great King. And do not swear by your head, for you cannot make one hair white or black. Let your word be "Yes, Yes" or "No, No"; anything more than this comes from the evil one.

—Matthew 5:33-37

Does Jesus render all oaths and vows impermissible for his followers? There have been Christians like the Mennonites and the Quakers who thought this to be the case. Christians need not take vows because our whole lives, under the second commandment, are a vow to be trusted. It ought to be vanity, using the Lord's name frivolously, to ask Christians to swear by God because it ought to be self-evident that all our words are spoken in the fear of the Lord.

Calvin argues for the use of oaths in only the most extreme circumstances. He suggests we should strive for simplicity of speech, particularly where there is use of God's name:

> Let us always follow this rule: to have the simplicity in our speech to say: "It is so," assuring ourselves that whatever is advantageous is evil and condemned by law whenever we take the name of God in vain. And in fact we can also see that there is a twofold evil in all superfluous oaths and in those in which the name of God is not at all honored as it deserves. For if anyone thus carelessly uses it at random, it is a sign that he hardly takes account of what he is saying. And then from whence does that proceed if it isn't from the fact that men are so lying and so full of fraud that when they speak to each other, no one can believe what the other says to him. Indeed it proceeds from perversity and malice. For when God gave us a tongue, it was in part for the purpose of communicating to one another, for it is like the messenger of the heart, for by means of it we express what we have conceived in our minds. Thus we see that superfluous oaths have proceeded from the disloyalty of men. And it is hardly necessary to inquire further, or to make an exhaustive study, for we can each testify to it. Whatever the case, let us learn to use [our tongue] in such sobriety as God commands. Thus let us not swear without purpose and unless we are required. (*Sermons on the Ten Commandments*, 87-88)

Simplicity of speech is a skill that is acquired by acknowledging the true God. It is not something to be had by trying hard to hold our tongues, but rather by being inculcated into a community where we learn and relearn that the world is sustained by God, not by our clever talk. In a society awash in words, constantly bombarded by commercials and advertisements, presidential press conferences, government statements, and data overload on the information highway, we become anesthetized by the verbiage of illusion. Our politicians lie, not necessarily because they are evil, but because it is the kind of speech that we desire. Political debate is reduced to thirty-second sound bites, because we couldn't stand a more truthful rendition of our situation.

The church has quite a witness to bear in a society of deceitful speech through our conversation with one another. If we can speak truthfully to God before the altar, perhaps we can speak truthfully to one another around a conference table. Our theology of speech arises from our theology of the church. All talk has as its goal the edification of the church:

Let all of us speak the truth to our neighbors, for we are members of one another. . . . Let no evil talk come out of your mouths, but only what is useful for building up, as there is need, so that your words may give grace to those who hear. . . . Be imitators of God, as beloved children, and live in love, as Christ loved us and gave himself up for us, a fragrant offering and sacrifice to God.

—Ephesians 4:25, 29; 5:1-2

A youth director told us, "When we take kids out for a retreat or on a mission trip we have one important rule—NO MEDIA." No media? No magazines, no radios or TVs, no recorders and no players. "It usually takes us at least twenty-four hours to wean them off the stuff. Only then can we do anything important with them." It was like she was talking about getting them off drugs.

When we were in seminary we were told that preaching was dead, that it could not compete with the slick showbiz of TV. Yet some years ago, when the effect of TV on people was studied, a high degree of distrust was found. When people watched TV, they were not thinking, *This is great!* They were thinking, *I am probably hearing a lie.* Having been lied to so much by the tube, they defended themselves against its incursions.

This may be a golden opportunity for the church to rediscover the holiness of preaching, the wonder of a human being authorized by the church and God to stand up and, with simplicity and candor, speak the truth in love.

After the O. J. Simpson acquittal, one of us preached a sermon in which he stooped to sarcasm and ridicule of the American legal system. An attorney emerged from church telling the preacher, "We deserved that. Thank God there's still a church with enough guts to make fun of us! For God's sake, keep telling the truth!"

For God's sake, indeed.

We also recall the woman who sent us a tape of her pastor's sermons in a little Presbyterian church in South Carolina during the war with Iraq. She wanted us to hear his condemnation of the war, his call for repentance.

"This is typical of what we get most any Sunday," she said with some pride. "You can't get this sort of stuff just anywhere around here. You have to get up, get dressed, and come to church for words like this."

It is a marvelous gift to be part of a people who, because we have learned faithfully to use God's name, are thus enabled to call what we do and do not do by their proper names.

Chapter Three

> *Remember the sabbath day, and keep it holy. Six days you shall labor and do all your work. But the seventh day is a sabbath to the LORD your God; you shall not do any work —you, your son or your daughter, your male or female slave, your livestock, or the alien resident in your towns. For in six days the LORD made heaven and earth, the sea, and all that is in them, but rested the seventh day; therefore the LORD blessed the sabbath day and consecrated it.*
>
> —Exodus 20:8-11

The Third Commandment

Americans are working longer than ever, spending more hours at work than a decade ago. We are a nation with a can-do attitude. That means the third commandment is ruthlessly countercultural. As Christians, we must recover the significance of withdrawing from American culture on Sundays. Sabbath is not just about taking time off, it is retaking time, taking time in God's name, which is no small witness to a world deluded into thinking that time is its own.

Last year Wellesley College hosted a conference to discuss religious diversity, religious pluralism. Representatives from many faiths were there in an effort to better understand one another. The conference began at 11:00 A.M. on Sunday. That Christians participated in the conference without complaint is another sign of how deeply accommodating we have become to our culture, how we have lost the sense of distinctiveness that would make Christians interesting to understand in the first place. We confess with some shame that commencement at Duke University takes place on Sunday morning.

Our time is not our own. Like life itself, time is a gift of God, thus it is accountable to God. Having created time, the sun, the moon, the seasons (Genesis 1), having given us time, God has much to say in how we use time and how we allow time to use us. Therefore this command is longer than the other commands, because God takes the time to place the command in the story of Creation.

The Sabbath is the major way in which Israel is identified as Israel. To "remember" the Sabbath is more than to recall an idea in our heads. It is also to bend our lives to the contour of the command, to worship, which is a reminder that the commandment itself is a form of worship. There can be no distinctions between "worship" and "ethics," because God has given us the time to worship God faithfully.

In Genesis, work is presented as a curse, a hard and difficult aspect of life in a fallen world (Genesis 3:17-20). Hard, grueling labor was not what God intended for the world at Creation. A good garden was what God intended. What God got, due to our sin, was a thorn-choked world of weeds, rocks, and dust that would yield its fruit only with hard work.

So Sabbath is a great gift of God to humanity. "The sabbath was made for humankind, and not humankind for the sabbath," said Jesus (Mark 2:27).

The reason given for the Sabbath is that even God rested one day out of seven after Creation (Genesis 2:2). Thus, Sabbath is the goal of Creation. This means that keeping Sabbath is a matter for the whole world, not just Israel, so even animals and strangers are to enjoy it. Furthermore, Sabbath is tied to Creation in that, in resting, God signaled the goodness of divine creativity in the world, the finished quality of the world. When God paused to call creation "good" (Genesis 1:10, 31), God was enjoying his sovereignty. God was saying, "I am God, and I can create a world and its wonderful creatures without being diminished as God." Built right into the core of our lives is this gracious rhythm of work and rest, activity and reflection. So to keep Sabbath is to be in step with the way God intends the world to work, it is to participate in an act of "re-creation" in which we are put back in touch with the way in which God intends for life to be enjoyed. Sabbath is not the joy of not doing work, rather Sabbath is perfect work, the end of work, the end of it all.

That Sabbath names the seventh day of creation is a reminder that the commandments are not just about "morality," but involve claims about the way things are. To rightly know the truth about the world, we must worship God. And to be so formed is to understand why we must tell one another the truth. Not to speak truthfully is to fail to live according to our true nature—that is, creatures who have life as a gift from a gracious Creator.

Sabbath so understood is cosmic, but then so is the Resurrection. That our time was changed by the Resurrection means no subjectivist accounts of the Resurrection are truthful; that is, that Resurrection names but the vivid memory of Jesus in the disciples. Rather, Resurrection is about the reordering of time, the redemption of creation from sin and death. The Decalogue, under the dispensation of the new age begun in the Resurrection, becomes life-giving because we can now see the commandment in the light of the Resurrection. The world is a matter of God's work rather than our anxious striving. Christians can live righteously, nonviolently, even though our living so, at least from the world's perspective, is not "productive."

Sabbath keeping is a sign of trust that God governs this world, therefore we don't have to work to make things come out right. God welcomes our labors, but our contributions to creation have their limits. Even God trusted all that God had created enough to be confident that the world would continue while God rested. So should we. Unlike the Greek god Atlas, we need not bear the world on our shoulders. Like God, we can stay away from the office for a day of rest in the conviction that the world will not go to hell simply because we are at rest.

It may seem odd to speak of resting as an ethical activity. Yet consider how much havoc we have wreaked in the world with our ceaseless work and striving. We get organized, make plans, move forward, begin to build. Babel is frequently the result of human busyness (Genesis 11), Calvary too. On the Sabbath we stop and take stock. We find ourselves falling back upon the Everlasting Arms, resting upon the promises of God not to desert us, not to allow chaos to overwhelm. It takes a people confident in God to rest.

Karl Barth opened his extended discussion of Christian ethics with consideration of the holy day:

> The Sabbath commandment explains all the other commandments, or all the other forms of the one commandment. It is thus to be placed at their head. By demanding man's abstention and resting from his own works, it explains that the commanding God, who has created man and commissioned him to do his work, is the God who is gracious to man in Jesus Christ. Thus it points him away from everything that he himself can will and achieve and back to what God is for him and will do for him. It reminds man of God's plan for him, of the fact that He has already carried it out, and that in His revelation He will execute both His will with him and His work for him and toward him. It points him to the Yes which the Creator has spoken to him, his creature, and which He has continued and at last definitely acknowledges, which He has made true and proved true once and for all in Jesus Christ. (*Church Dogmatics* 3/4, 53)

Barth was right to make the third commandment the command that shapes how we understand the other commandments. The third commandment is a reminder that we have been created for no higher purpose than the worship of God.

The old Westminster Confession asked, "What is the chief end of humanity?"

The correct answer: "To glorify God and to enjoy him forever."

Our lives are but a celebration of the One who graciously makes possible for us to be. Sabbath rest testifies to the complete goodness of God's creativity. As Barth said, "In deference to God, to the heart and meaning of his work, there must be from time to time an interruption, a rest, a deliberate non-continuation, a temporal pause, to reflect on God and His work and to participate consciously in the salvation provided by Him to be awaited from Him" (*Church Dogmatics* 3/4, 50).

Sabbath is much more than doing nothing. We are enjoined this day to remember, recall, recollect, and re-create. We are not simply to remember that we ought to keep the Sabbath, but we are to remember who God is—active and loving, resourceful beyond our actions and resources. We are to remember who we are—gifted, sustained and blessed beyond our striving and achieving.

Aquinas claimed that one of the reasons why God gave us the third commandment is that "the Holy Spirit saw that in the future some men would say that the world had always existed." They would claim that the world was a self-sufficient entity with no need of continual divine nurturance.

In the last days scoffers will come, scoffing and indulging their own lusts and saying, "Where is the promise of his coming? For ever since our ancestors died, all things continue as they were from the beginning of creation!" They deliberately ignore this fact, that by the word of God heavens existed long ago and our earth was formed out of water and by means of water.

—2 Peter 3:3-5

God is rest. Rest is not only God's perfect activity through the shared life of the Trinity, but it is also testimony that the true God is vulnerable. The pharaohs of the world are loathe to admit vulnerability or need. The true God is so serene and confident in his reign that this God *can* afford to take time off from creation to rest.

Accordingly the Sabbath has striking economic implications. It is for the rich, who are often oppressed and harassed in their riches and their accumulation. It is for the poor, who are often overburdened in their work. Even animals are given rest. On a weekly basis, the ambiguity of work is brought to the community's attention. We experience, just for a day, a world where there are not such great gaps between rich and poor. In our world, only the rich get time off. The poor have to work two jobs to make ends meet. But on Sabbath, all this is rectified, judged, and rearranged, and we are reminded that our economic systems are not divinely ordained. We create capitalism or socialism. God created and commanded Sabbath.

The Sabbath, as we have already noted, calls attention to the cosmic nature of our salvation. God loves not only us; God loves the whole creation, even the animals. In the third commandment, we are no better than the animals. In fact, the commandment reminds us that we *are* animals, and like the animals, we need rest. At the heart of God's intentions for all creatures is rest. This commandment, as much as any other, shows Israel's wonderful inclination to link the commands of God to concrete, everyday, ordinary social realities. With this commandment, the Ten Commandments move from declarations about the nature of God toward human relationships. With the Sabbath command, we are moving into that workaday world of pots and pans and genitals, naming that world, not as a place of ceaseless striving, but as a world put into proper perspective by the command of God. Thus Revelation claims that our goal in life is eternal worship, continual Sabbath, where humanity will join all creatures in doing nothing better than singing praise to the Lamb:

Then I heard every creature in heaven and on earth and under the earth and in the sea, and all that is in them, singing,

> *"To the one seated on the throne*
> *and to the Lamb*
> *be blessing and honor and glory*
> *and might*
> *forever and ever!"*
> —Revelation 5:13

The Third Commandment in Christian Life

The Sabbath is about time, about the way that God moves in time, not above it. God constantly makes promises to us, projecting our relationship with God into the future by keeping those promises. God continually (as in the third commandment) bids us to remember, basing our present on God's past dealings with us. The goal of Sabbath is therefore not to rescue us from time, suspending us in some eternality above time, but rather it is a reminder to redeem our time—past, present, and future—as God's.

As Abraham Joshua Heschel puts the matter:

> Judaism is a religion of time aimed at the sanctification of time. Unlike the space-blinded man to whom time is unvaried, iterative, homogeneous, to whom all hours are alike, qualitiless, empty shells, the Bible senses the diversified character of time. There are no two hours alike. Every hour is unique and only one given at the moment, exclusive and endlessly precious. Judaism teaches us to be attached to holiness in time, to be attached to sacred events, to learn how to consecrate sanctuaries that emerge from the magnificent stream of a year. Sabbaths are our great cathedrals; and our holy of holies is a shrine that neither the Romans nor the Germans were able to burn; a shrine that even apostasy cannot easily obliterate: the Day of Atonement. According to the ancient Rabbis, it is not the observance of the Day of Atonement but the Day itself, the "essence of the Day," which, with man's repentance, atones for sins of man. (*The Sabbath*, 8)

Later we shall learn to sanctify, to render liturgical, our families, our marriages, our property. Here, in this commandment, we are told how to sanctify time. We learn to be in time as God's creatures. In worship we take time, or more accurately, in worship God gives us time.

Christians believe that Sabbath has been forever changed through the Resurrection. Jesus was raised on the eighth day, becoming for us a new creation, giving us back time in a way we would not have had without God's raising Jesus from the dead. Just as God entrusted to Israel the Sabbath so that the world might know God's intentions for Creation, so Christians worship on the day of the Resurrection, thereby signaling that God's promise to Israel has gone to all the world. All are created to share the rest, the salvation, that comes from worship of the true God. In our Sunday worship Christians serve the world by showing the world that God has not left us alone and that we have good work to do. In its Greek derivation, *liturgy* means "the work of the people." Worship is the work God does with us to show the world a manner of life that could not be known had not God vindicated Jesus.

Sunday is therefore a day set apart whereby Christians are reminded that they are set apart as a people. To be set apart is to be made holy, to be sanctified. Contemporary Christians often fear to be classified as such, thinking with false modesty that they should be "no better than everybody else." Christians, however, are called to be holy, to find in the commandments a life worth living, a life of joy. Moreover, we believe that if our lives manifest the joy of living obedient to the commandments, others will be attracted. For they too were created by God and are meant to live by the commandments. Christian evangelism is quite simple—others are attracted because they see how we love one another. We have time for such love, even to tell one another the truth because we are a Sabbath people.

Just as the Sabbath is a distinguishing characteristic of Jews, setting them apart, keeping them together as Jews, so Sunday is a visible mark of Christians. The Sabbath is visible enactment and witness that Jews need not live by the defining characteristics of other peoples, striving, building, and establishing, but instead live in grateful, relaxed confidence in the true God's ability to have and to preserve a family. We gather to hear the Word we could not have heard had it not been spoken; we gather to share a meal among those who could not be our sisters and brothers had we not all been adopted in Christ. Sometimes our worship practice is criticized as being too passive, all sitting and listening and not enough action. But we need to recover the sense of how some of the most important work we do is sitting and listening to Scripture, taking time to sit and listen to a sermon, to be fed. In simply withdrawing from what the world considers its important business, in taking time to do nothing but worship in a world at war, in celebrating an order of worship in a world of chaos, Christians are making a most political statement. It takes courage to take time to worship God in a world where we are constantly told that it is up to us to do right, or right won't be done. As we shall see in the next commandment, it takes courage to take time to have children in a world that loves them not.

In the high school one of us attended there was a young man who was a star on the basketball team. He was a wonderful defensive player, a key to the whole team's success. If the team played anytime during the week, he was there and he invariably led the team to victory. But if the team played on Friday, he was absent. After a Friday night game, the team would gather at his home and give him a play-by-play report on the game, a game that was often lost because of his absence.

His absence on the Sabbath was a witness that something else had hold of his time, something even more important than basketball. He was different. He had something to do with his time, a calling, a commitment, which made him better than the rest of us. He was a Jew.

In the Eucharist, we remember, we "do this in remembrance" that our time is God's. Jesus has commanded us to gather often and to break bread in remembrance of him. Catholics speak of this as their "Sunday Obligation." *The Catechism of the Catholic Church (1994)* says,

> The Sunday Eucharist is the foundation and confirmation of all Christian practice. For this reason the faithful are obliged to participate in the Eucharist on days of obligation, unless excused for a serious reason (for example, illness, the care of infants) as dispensed by their own pastor. Those who deliberately fail in this obligation commit a grave sin. (527)

Obligation sounds to Protestant ears like legalism. We believe there is much to be said for such "legalism." We do not go to church to be renewed for the demands of a busy week, but rather we go to church as service to God, service that is pleasing to ourselves and God, but even when it is not pleasing to us, it is necessary to the world's salvation. By ordering our lives on Sunday so that worship is primary, we witness to the world that this is God's good time.

Not all work can be avoided on the Sabbath. Aquinas said that we must avoid all "servile" work, by which he means all bodily work. Priests work at the altar, said Aquinas, but that is free so all work done on the Sabbath ought to be free, that is, activity for the upbuilding of the community. How to distinguish between bodily and free work is an ongoing task, but Aquinas's suggestion that presiding at the altar is free work is a fruitful place to begin analogical discrimination.

At the least, Sabbath ought to be an occasion when we avoid making unnecessary demands upon others. Sabbath keeping is a defense against the exploitative, purely pragmatic, and ruthlessly utilitarian tendencies of the world. Like the Jubilee year in which Israel was to free slaves and land, so the Sabbath ought to be our time to enjoy one another. We know a family who for years has kept Sabbath. Their rule is that you can do no work on the Sabbath unless it is a joy. If planting bulbs in the yard is work, then it must wait until Monday. If it is a joy, then it is Sabbath work.

One of us was raised in Texas, where there is a wonderful institution known as "Juneteenth." On June 19, news of the Emancipation Proclamation reached Texas. June 19 became the day on which African Americans, with no legal recourse, simply refused to show up for work. Whites might not have liked it, but there was nothing they could do about it. They simply accepted "Juneteenth" as a holiday.

The Christian Sabbath is Juneteenth. It is when Christians perform one of our most radical, countercultural, peculiarly defining acts—we simply refuse to show up for work. It is how we put the world in its place. It is how we take over the world's time and help to make it God's time. It is how we get over our amnesia and recover our memory of how we got here, who we are, and in whose service we are called. Memory is hard for us, not because we have got to resuscitate in memory a dead Jesus, but rather because we become distracted from the joyful truth that Jesus is resurrected, present among us in time, for all time.

Thus Calvin speaks of the Sabbath as a model of civil order, the time when we are trained for our true service to God. "And what is this order? It is to assemble ourselves in the name of God" (*Sermons,* 108). We need to take time to separate ourselves from the world's disorder so that the world might see true order.

When the Scripture speaks to us about being sanctified before God, it means for us to separate ourselves from everything contrary to his service. But now where will one find such purity? We are in the world and we know that in this world there is only perversity and malice. . . . We cannot worship him in purity, unless we separate ourselves from opposing pollutions, or until what belongs to our nature is abolished. (*Sermons,* 99)

Political holiness is not simply obeying this or that law. Christian politics is constituted by the worship of the true God found in Jesus Christ. It is politics that assumes we have all the time in the world, eternity, in a world of deep injustice and pain, to take time to worship. In an unjust world, we either want anxiously to take time into our hands and right the wrong on our terms or, worse, to acquiesce to the injustice, giving it sovereignty, assuming that God cannot or will not work in time to do a new thing. Sunday worship is thus a radical protest from the world's time, a time when we literally take time to rejoice that in Jesus Christ God has made our time his own. We are given on the Sabbath a glimpse of eternity, an experience of what God means for all time where God has "blessing and honor and glory and might forever and ever!" (Revelation 5:13).

Christian time is not the world's time. This is clear by the very fact that the Christian year is not the world's year. The Christian year begins with Advent and Christmas, continues with Lent and Easter, and climaxes with Pentecost and the birth of the church. That is the time that constitutes the politics of Christian living. That is the time that constitutes the very being of the world. So if the Fourth of July is more important in your church than Pentecost, you will begin to understand how the commandments constitute a politics just to the extent that the church has been corrupted.

Chapter Four

> *Honor your father and your mother, so that your days may be long in the land that the LORD your God is giving you.*
>
> – Exodus 20:12

The Fourth Commandment

"Which act of worship do you find the most strange, the most radically odd of all that we do on a Sunday morning?" a group of college students was asked.

One student answered immediately, "It's when, just after we all get there, right at the beginning, during the first song, there is that big parade . . ."

"Procession?"

"Yeah, procession. And at the end of the choir, just before the ministers, somebody always brings in that old, big, great big book."

"The Bible?"

"Yeah, the Bible. That's odd."

Then we realized she was absolutely right and wonderfully perceptive. That late-twentieth century people would gather, that an ancient, disordered text from another time and culture would be produced with such ceremony, opened, and then submitted to, is quite weird, even subversive. We normally do not treat our parents so kindly.

In one sense the modern world began as Freud's attempt to kill his father ended in the killing of God. Freud taught us to believe that we ought to hate the ones who produced us, to render ourselves into our own creators through therapy. We so want to be gods unto ourselves.

Yet nothing is quite as ontologically revealing as our belly button. This is only one of the teachings of the fourth commandment. By noting that we are creatures, creations of mothers and fathers, the Decalogue tells us that we have life as a gift. We are begotten, not manufactured. Someone even changed our diapers, our first hint of what grace must be like. No wonder some of us despise our parents, for they are a visible, ever-present reminder that we were created, that the significance of our lives is not exclusively self-derived. Luther, with characteristic vitality, put it this way:

> If we had no father and mother, we should wish, on account of the commandments, that God would set up a block or a stone which we might call father and mother. How much more, when he has given us living parents, should we be happy to show them honor and obedience. For we know that it is highly pleasing to divine Majesty and all the angels, that it vexes all the devils, and, besides, that it is the greatest work that we can do, next to the sublime worship of God described in the previous commandments. . . . For God has exalted this estate of parents above all others; indeed, he has appointed it to be his representative on earth. (*The Large Catechism,* 26)

Gratitude is thus the faithful response to the discovery that we are creatures. We have not been created to stand alone, but rather to need one another. Nurtured within someone's womb, the most dependent of all creatures at birth and the least adept at fending for ourselves for the longest time, our attachments to our parents remind us that life is gift rather than possession. Each of us has been parented. No matter how old we become, no matter how many children we ourselves may have, we never get over being children of God and our parents.

As we have noted, the Decalogue is often divided into the opening commands, which counsel love of God, and the "second table," which deals with love of neighbor. The second set is said to be about ethics while the first table is assumed to be about religion.

By now we hope you see how this division, while understandable, is artificial and misleading. Aquinas said that the commands of God are not only rightly numbered but rightly ordered. It is not accidental that the command to observe the Sabbath is followed by the command to honor father and mother. Even as the third commandment tells us that we must live in time as a gift, rather than as an arena of our achievements and assertions, so the fourth commandment commands us to live as those who know their very being is a gift. Our lives are not self-derived. The self-made man or woman is a lie.

How we ought to live with one another—in families—is derived from how we worship God:

And this is his commandment, that we should believe in the name of his Son Jesus Christ and love one another, just as he has commanded us. All who obey his commandments abide in him, and he abides in them.   —1 John 3:23-24

Thus in moving to the sphere of human relationships, the Decalogue builds on its assertions for proper worship of God. The sort of love with which we are to love the neighbor is the same by which we love God. If we can learn to forgive our parents, forgiving our next-door neighbor ought to be easy. Not only is it that we love because God first loved us, but also that we are to love our parents (according to the fourth commandment) in the manner that we love God. It is rather surprising, after first affirming the unique majesty and sovereignty of God, that the commandments now tell us to obey our parents as we obey God.

Calvin qualifies this command by saying that

we are bidden to obey our parents only "in the Lord" (Eph. 6:1). . . . For they sit in that place to which they have been advanced by the Lord, who shares with them a part of his honor. Therefore, the submission paid to them ought to be a step toward honoring that highest Father. Hence, if they spur us to transgress the law, we have a perfect right to regard them not as parents, but as strangers who are trying to lead us away from obedience to our true Father. So should we act toward princes, lords, and every kind of superiors. It is unworthy and absurd for their eminence so to prevail as to pull down the loftiness of God. On the contrary, their eminence depends upon God's loftiness and ought to lead us to it. (*Institutes of the Christian Religion*, 403-4)

We admit that sometimes the commandments of the second table are read so as to underwrite the practices of conventional social arrangements. Does this commandment make of the family an idol, demanding that we give parents glory that ought only be given to God? The family can be a terribly hurtful, increasingly violent place for many children and women. Is it wise to tell the most vulnerable to honor the more powerful?

We must take care in how we interpret this commandment, particularly in the context of the current debate over family values.

First, let us admit that, in this culture, *any* admission of dependency—that is, any position that seems to be constrained, without freedom of choice—is always regarded as potentially detrimental to our highest ideal for modern humanity: the free, unattached, sovereign, choosing individual. Isn't this commandment an invitation for already vulnerable, dependent children to encourage their parents to be tyrants?

We suspect that some contemporary critics of the family who accuse the church of promoting "idolatry of the family" do so in the typically modern interest of freeing us from all social attachments so that we may be attached only to the self in order for the state to have its way with us. Contemporary democracies have found that people are much more manageable by the state when they are told that they are individuals who have no responsibilities to anyone other than to themselves. People who have a home and parents at least have some means of possibly resisting the almighty state and its economy.

However, any limitation on the fourth commandment arises not primarily from our determination to be free of idolatrous attachments, but rather out of our obedience to God. Jesus confused his parents and disobeyed them in order to be obedient to God's will. The only episode we have from Jesus' childhood is that trouble at the Temple when Jesus seems to mistreat his parents (Luke 2:41-51) by staying behind at Jerusalem in order to debate theology with the Bible scholars. From this we infer that parents are to be honored as they honor God. Parents are to be obeyed as they obey God. Each commandment qualifies and interprets every other commandment. Those who expect to be honored by their children's keeping of the fourth commandment must themselves keep the Ten Commandments.

Moreover we must remember that this commandment is not addressed to young children but to adult children, which is all of us, eventually. Adults, who are all children of someone, are the audience for this address. To "honor your father and mother" is a claim about who we are as creatures, not just when we are young, but always.

Jesus dared to use even so risky a social setting as the family for some of his most radical teaching about the nature of God:

Then Jesus said, "There was a man who had two sons. The younger of them said to his father, 'Father, give me the share of the property that will belong to me.' So he divided his property between them. A few days later the younger son gathered all he had and traveled to a distant country, and there he squandered his property in dissolute living."

—Luke 15:11-13

So this commandment is not about justifying something called family values, as if the family is good in and of itself. Nothing is absolutely good. Everything is relative, relative to the Trinity. The world is good only as it relates to the will and wisdom of a gracious God. This commandment is a reminder to adult parents that the children for whom they have responsibility, just as their own parents once had responsibility for them, are due to be nurtured in a manner that they may be glad to be a child of God. We ought to honor our parents, said Aquinas, for it was they who first taught us to worship God. From them, we caught the first inkling of what it meant to be loved, sought, sacrificed for, selflessly cared for, and what it means to be dependent on another for life itself.

Furthermore, this commandment reminds parents that God is the significance of their parenthood. Parenting is a gift of God in which some of us are given the grace to discover our lives enmeshed in webs of gift and responsibility that are life-giving and life-sustaining. God, having enjoyed primal creativity, offers this gift to the woman and the man, telling us to "be fruitful and multiply" (Genesis 1:28), which is not only the very first of God's commands to humanity, but one of the most delightful in the fulfilling! Parenthood is thus a high vocation, one worthy of our honor, for it is participation by some of the faithful in the responsibility and creativity through which God keeps the world as God's world and creation continues.

The Fourth Commandment in Christian Life

Our parents, in faithfulness, become for us our first priests, ministering to us by telling us the stories of God, instructing us in God's law, modeling for us how to obey God and thus to be happy. Without their guidance, we would not know that God is the source of our lives, we would have no way of knowing that God has a claim upon us, that we are called. Our belly buttons keep reminding us that all we have and all we are is a gift.

Therefore children are not given to parents for our pleasure and amusement, though, by God's grace, amid the burdens of childbearing, children are often great pleasure and delightful amusement. Children are given to us in order that we might be brought closer to God. In fulfilling our parental vocation, we find out that we are better people than we would have been if we had not become parents. We begin to order our lives more faithfully so that we can be good parents. We can think of no better example of the way in which there is no difference between law and gift. In being obedient parents, we are given the gift of obedience.

Let it also be noted that parents are not given to children merely for security and adoration, though parents do often succeed in providing us more than a modicum of security in our early years, and usually a mother believes in her child when no one else will. Parents are there to keep teaching us that we are here as a gift. As parents age, a wonderful reversal of roles takes place. Adult children are given the opportunity to order their lives and resources in behalf of their aging parents. We who have received care from parents now get to care for them. We who have had our diapers changed by parents, without feeling at the time any gratitude, get to offer our thanks by changing their diapers. Honoring our fathers and mothers, obeying this commandment, becomes a very mundane, practical, bodily matter in the extended-care ward of a nursing home.

Our notions of honorable fathers and mothers flow from what we believe about God. It is not (per Freud) that we humans have an infantile need for a cosmic father so we project our human experiences of fatherhood upon some contrived God the Father. It was Jesus who taught us in the Lord's Prayer to call God Father. Any notions we have of human fatherhood are derived from Jesus' revelation of the nature of God, not vice versa. All biological fatherhood is judged and relativized by Jesus' naming of God as Father. Jesus told a wonderful story about a father with two sons (Luke 15) who had to go through hell in order to have a family. Jesus himself is the very embodiment of the Father's relentless determination to have a family. Thus, Jesus rearranges and judges our notions of "mother" and "father" by his own redemptive words and work.

So Aquinas observed that, in the church, some men are called "father," not because they generate children, but because they deserve reverence (*The Catechetical Instructions*, 91). We call the apostles and the early churchmen "fathers" because of their exemplification of faith. In the church, mothers and fathers are not made through biology but through baptism. We are supposed to look through the institution of the human family toward *the* family, the church. The church ought to honor the saints in such a way that our life together as the church is both call and judgment upon our biological families.

Thus, when a child is baptized, it is important that the church make clear that the whole church is sponsoring and taking responsibility for the faith of the child, not just the child's biological parents. "Parent" names the Christian vocation that fosters the emerging child in the faith. For most of us, parents are the first evangelists, the first to speak and to embody the gospel for us. All people in the church, whether they have biological children or not, are called to care for children through baptism. In baptism, many are rescued from the clutches and limitations of their biological families and adopted into the only family big enough, and true enough, to be called "family," the church.

This is the major reason why the church should be suspicious of secular acclamation of family values. The church opposes any power that claims to care for children in any way that qualifies the church's parenting. The human nuclear family, or any other human configuration called family, is to receive its significance and to be held accountable to our primary family, the family of faith called church.

Expect Christians, therefore, to be critical of state-run institutions for children such as the public schools. Expect us to resist any scheme of child-rearing that makes God less than authoritative for our children's lives. However, expect Christians to honor those civil authorities and social institutions that provide for the stability and support of the family whereby we are allowed to be faithful to our obligation to raise children in the faith. A basic reason for historic Christian criticism of capitalism as an economic system is that system's penchant for putting stress upon families. Most American families suffer today not from the call for gay rights, but because they have no means of resisting the burden of constant acquisitiveness and consumerism, the sickness some have called "affluenza." Socialism, as an economic-political system, in subordinating family to the care of the state, carries with it its own challenges to the family. The economic order is never a good in itself but rather is to be judged by its ability to provide those goods whereby the lives of children and parents flourish. Therefore, in honoring those civil servants who are in authority over us, due to the fourth commandment, we also remind them that they are in authority as those who are under the judgment of

God. The primary motivation for Christian critique and reform of social orders is our obedience to God rather than to humanity (Acts 5:29).

One can see from our discussion of the fourth commandment that Christians recognize no distinction between "public" and "private." The American family has been "privatized," which means that the family is alleged to be that sphere of psychological relations and personal opinions, a "haven in a heartless world," safe from the public sphere. So students go to school to be educated in what really matters, the facts—that public, socially significant knowledge by which they will gain power as this society defines power. They retreat to the family for those skills that are personal, private, and irrelevant to the facts of life. The family gets demoted to little more than a sanctuary from some of the hurt of the real world.

The fourth commandment, in putting family squarely within the sphere of public responsibility and politics, refuses to make family private. Christians therefore can think of few more politically charged debates than an argument over what we do with our children.

Hierarchy is built into the ways Jews and Christians live in the world. In honoring mothers and fathers, in submitting to God as the Father, we are trained in a manner of subjection that a democratic society will consider odd. Democracy tends to delude us into thinking that we may live our lives as if no authority need be acknowledged unless it personally suits us. In a democracy we are free to choose to whom we shall submit. We therefore tend to think of God as someone we have chosen, a democratically elected leader, the great liberal benefactor in the sky. No, God is our Creator and the One who has redeemed our lives through the cross and resurrection of Jesus Christ. Thus God is the only One who can command obedience.

Yet, in modernity, any exercise of authority is bound to feel authoritarian. At the dawn of a new millennium, we are people who have no experience in truthful authority. Nowhere is this seen more graphically than in the anarchy exhibited in our children's lives. Parents lacking any sense of authority even in their own lives raise their children to "make up their own minds," which means our children are robbed of minds worth making up. We and our children become slaves to our own disordered desires.

As Luther saw it, the absence of a truthful hierarchy leads to chaotic anarchy:

> If we ever let ourselves be persuaded that works of obedience are so pleasing to God and have so rich reward, we shall be simply overwhelmed with our blessings and we shall have all that our hearts desire. But God's Word and commandments are despised, as if they came from some loutish peddler. Let us see, though, whether you are the man to defy him. How difficult do you think it will be for him to pay you back? You will live much better with God's favor, peace, and blessing than you will with the disfavor and misfortune. Why, do you think, is the world now so full of unfaithfulness, shame, misery, and murder? It is because everyone wishes to be his own master, be free of all authority, care nothing for anyone, and do whatever he pleases. So God punishes one knave by means of another. When you defraud or despise your master, another person comes along and treats you likewise. Indeed, in your household you must suffer ten times as much wrong from your own wife, children, or servants. (*The Large Catechism*, 30)

Though written in the sixteenth century, how well Luther's description of a world where there is no valid authority and hierarchy describes our own day. If we will not honor our mothers and fathers, we will still obey someone, who too often turns out to be the state or "the business." Fearing no rightful authority results in our fearing everyone and most particularly ourselves.

But the fourth commandment ends not in threat of punishment, but in promise of blessing. It promises us that our "days will be long" in the land that God has given us. We are given the blessing of time and place, so by God's grace we have the place and the time we need to care for children and for parents. Parenting requires such patience because children take so much time. We have made time into a commodity, a scarce commodity at that (so we speak of "spending time" and "wasting time"). Here, in this commandment, time is gift, as well as place, so that we might have the routine, the predictability, the time, and the space needed to be joyfully obedient to the God who has given us meaningful ministry to perform in the meantime.

Honoring parents is also a reminder that as a Sabbath people we have been given the time to live by memory. Put more strongly, Christians are constituted by memory—"Do this in remembrance of me." We therefore live through the memory of those whom Christ has made through body and blood. We have tried in the very way we have written this book, that is, by learning from Aquinas, Luther, and Calvin, to manifest our indebtedness to those who have gone before. The first attitudes of Christians toward those who preceded us, thereby making us possible, are humility and thankfulness. Such attitudes do not mean uncritical acceptance of everything they said, but rather even our criticism must be a mode of honoring.

Of course the problem with names like Aquinas, Luther, and Calvin is that they are too well known. Most Christians of the past seem lost in obscurity. But we do not believe that to be the case. Rather, we think they enjoy God as part of the communion of saints. That they do so means we have been given the time to live recognizing that their gift has made us safe.

If you are uneasy about this commandment's promise of blessing and reward for those who are obedient, get over it. It is either the good news or the bad news of the Decalogue that our actions have consequences. The Old Testament repeatedly asserts that certain conduct really does lead to long and happy lives. If we walk in this path rather than that one, our lives go better. God takes note of obedience and is willing to stoop even to reward. Even if few note the sacrificial care a woman gives her mother during her mother's last days on this earth, God notes. Even though the world will not reward her, God rewards. A long and happy life in a good place is the reward of a life well lived, and a life well lived is one obedient to the commandments of God.

Something about us would rather ascribe our lives to fate, good or bad luck, rather than obedient or disobedient conduct. We wonder "why bad things happen to good people" rather than be filled with wonderment for how, even in this disordered world, good things really do often happen to good people. Actions have consequences, and how we live makes a difference. Thus our being obedient, honoring our fathers and mothers, even though it was done in the worship of God rather than for expectation of reward, graciously ends for most of us in the reward of long and happy lives in the land that God has given us.

Chapter Five

> *You shall not murder.*
> – Exodus 20:13

The Fifth Commandment

Here is a commandment that is short, terse, to the point. Simple. The commandment's simplicity stands in contrast not only to the way we actually live, but also to the ongoing interpretation and debate expended by the church in its tireless efforts to have the fifth commandment say what we would like it to say. Such strenuous efforts at interpretation are understandable among those who live in the most violent culture ever created, North American democracy (if one just adds up the bodies of citizens killed by their fellow citizens, to say nothing of all the wars). More people have been killed by their own governments in this century even than in war. Standing here at the end of perhaps history's bloodiest century, this commandment ought to hit home.

In the Ten Commandments the actual Hebrew is not, "Thou shalt not kill." It is in fact, "Thou shalt not murder." So this is self-defense.

—John LeNoue, with wife Kaywin, born-again Christians explaining why they own handguns.[1]

In our attempts to weasel out of this command, we shall not be helped much by saying, "It doesn't really mean kill; it means murder." The Hebrew verb "to kill" does mean "murder" in certain contexts (cf. 1 Kings 21:19), but it can also refer to unintentional killing (Deuteronomy 4:41-42), as well as to execution of a duly convicted killer (Numbers 35:30). A sweeping, unconditional claim is being made on us. We do well to admit that it probably refers to any act of violence against someone under a wide range of circumstances, intentional and otherwise. "Murder" is too limited a term to encapsulate the concern of this commandment.

This insight ought to keep us uneasy before this commandment. When we take life for any reason we put ourselves in the place of God. We steal something that God created and that God owns. Stealing from a God who is "jealous" is a risky act. All life is God's. In the Bible, when killing is done, it is done under the agency of God, not by individuals or in service to the state, for only God is to kill and to make alive.

In saying that God's people are not to take life, the commandments put us at odds with every government on earth. Governments put themselves in the place of God and kill to defend themselves and their vaunted claims of sovereignty. With God's people, it is not to be so. Rather than ponder how we might skillfully reinterpret this command to suit present circumstances, our time might be better spent wondering how we might change the church to be the sort of place that produces and supports nonviolent people.

Jesus is no help in attempts to soften the force of this commandment. Indeed, in Matthew 5:21-26, Jesus expands the scope of the commandment to encompass even verbal abuse and angry outbursts against another. Rather than retribution or recompense, he demands reconciliation. Thus Jesus appears unwilling to be enlisted by those who teach "ethics" in an attempt to nuance this commandment. He takes a command that is already quite stark and makes it even more sweeping in its demand. Perhaps we ought to take Jesus' method of interpretation in Matthew 5:21-26 as a model for our interpretation—in Jesus the commandments are intensified, extended, expanded.

Do not think that I have come to abolish the law or the prophets; I have come not to abolish but to fulfill. For truly I tell you, until heaven and earth pass away, not one letter, not one stroke of a letter, will pass from the law until all is accomplished. Therefore, whoever breaks one of the least of these commandments, and teaches others to do the same, will be called least in the kingdom of heaven; but whoever does them and teaches them will be called great in the kingdom of heaven. For I tell you, unless your righteousness exceeds that of the scribes and Pharisees, you will never enter the kingdom of heaven.   —Matthew 5:17-20*

Luther said that the commandments are meant to strike us dead, to drive us into the hands of a merciful God. No other commandment does that better, particularly when heightened in intensity by Jesus in Matthew 5:21-26.

The demand that we live without killing makes no sense if God is not our Creator. Genesis tells us clearly that we were created to live without killing. Seldom noticed is the foundational claim that

God blessed them, and God said to them, "Be fruitful and multiply, and fill the earth and subdue it; and have dominion over the fish of the sea and over the birds of the air and over every living thing that moves upon the earth." God said, "See, I have given you every plant yielding seed that is upon the face of all the earth, and every tree with seed in its fruit; you shall have them for food. And to every beast of the earth, and to every bird of the air, and to everything that creeps on the earth, everything that has the breath of life, I have given every green plant for food." And it was so. God saw everything that he had made, and indeed, it was very good. And there was evening and there was morning, the sixth day.

—Genesis 1:28-31

It appears from this that God even expects animals to be vegetarians. God's intentions in creation are well depicted by the Quaker painter Edward Hicks in his paintings of *The Peaceable Kingdom,* where the wolf and the lamb lie together without the wolf devouring the lamb. That no animal is more deadly than humankind shows the mess we have made of God's intentions for the world.

After the great Flood, God blessed Noah and his family and commanded them again to be fruitful and multiply. Yet God also noted that something had gone terribly wrong in creation. Now the animals, which once conversed with humanity, living mutually in the good garden, fear and dread humanity because humanity lives by destroying life:

Every moving thing that lives shall be food for you; and just as I gave you the green plants, I give you everything. Only, you shall not eat flesh with its life, that is, its blood. For your own lifeblood I will surely require a reckoning: from every animal I will require it and from human beings, each one for the blood of another, I will require a reckoning for human life.

> *Whoever sheds the blood of a human,*
> *   by a human shall that person's blood be shed;*
> *for in his own image*
> *   God made humankind.*

—Genesis 9:3-6

This is the somber, sad, and disordered life we live. This was not the world as God intended, but the world we rendered in our sin. Now the Decalogue reminds us that we were not created to live by killing, not meant to live by the sacrifices of animals. Our practice of saying a grace before meals is our way of thanking God for the sacrifices of those whom we eat.

The rabbis often argue that Israel's complex food laws are

meant to make Israel vegetarian. Vegetarianism is not a peculiar practice for those who are especially sensitive toward the pain of animals. Rather, the refusal to eat meat is best based upon a joyful celebration of God's intentions for the world, intentions made manifest by Isaiah:

The wolf shall live with the lamb,
*   the leopard shall lie down with the kid,*
the calf and the lion and the fatling together,
*   and a little child shall lead them.*
The cow and the bear shall graze,
*   their young shall lie down together;*
*   and the lion shall eat straw like the ox. . . .*
They will not hurt or destroy
*   on all my holy mountain;*
for the earth will be full of the knowledge of the LORD
*   as the waters cover the sea.*

—Isaiah 11:6-9

Take this commandment as part of God's attempt to render an earth "full of the knowledge of the LORD," to remind us of that which, in our sin, we have forgotten, to draw our lives into that praise that transforms us into peaceable people who need not base our lives upon destruction and hurt of others.

So to ask of this commandment against killing, "Does this mean Christians shouldn't go to war?" is to reduce this joyful invitation to a legalistic requirement when it ought to be seen as an invitation to praise. In the cross of Christ, Christians are brought into a peaceful world where we are not forced to sustain our lives by killing. Jesus did not resort to killing, even self-defensive killing, to defend or to establish his kingdom, yet he was vindicated by God in his resurrection. He has shown us the way, the way of the cross, which defeats the world, but not on the world's terms. Without lying about the violence of the world, Christians are given a means of being free from the world's violence.

*Mainstream America is depending on you, counting on you, to draw
your sword and fight for them. These people have precious little time
or resources to battle misguided Cinderella attitudes, the fringe pro-
paganda of the homosexual coalition, the feminists who preach that
it's a divine duty for women to hate men, blacks who raise a militant
fist with one hand, while they seek preference with the other.*
— Charlton Heston, speaking to the National Rifle
Association, December 1997. Heston played
Moses in *The Ten Commandments*.[2]

Christians are not simply prohibited from killing, but also invited
to live in a way that does not force us to kill. As Aquinas noted,
Jesus tells us even to avoid anger (Matthew 5:21-22). Aquinas
does not mean that we are not to feel righteous indignation
against injustice, but rather that we are to develop among ourselves those virtues that free us from temptation to envy and self-
importance, which so often lead to presumptions that we have
been grievously wronged. Such bloated presumption too easily
leads to the killing called murder.

The Fifth Commandment in Christian Life

Some of the most eloquent words concerning the Fifth Commandment were written by Calvin:

The purpose of this commandment is: the Lord has bound
mankind together by a certain unity; hence each man ought to
concern himself with the safety of all. To sum up, then, all violence, injury, and any harmful thing at all that may injure our
neighbor's body are forbidden to us. We are accordingly commanded, if we find anything of use to us in saving our neighbor's
lives, faithfully to employ it; if there is anything that makes for their
peace, to see to it; if anything harmful, to ward it off; if they are
in any danger, to lend a helping hand. If you recall that God is so
speaking as Lawgiver, ponder at the same time that by this rule he

wills to guide your soul. For it would be ridiculous that he who looks upon the thoughts of the heart and dwells especially upon them, should instruct only the body in true righteousness. Therefore this law also forbids murder of the heart, and enjoins the inner intent to save a brother's life. The hand, indeed, gives birth to murder, but the mind when infected with anger and hatred conceives it. See whether you can be angry against your brother without burning with desire to hurt him. If you cannot be angry with him, then you cannot hate him, for hatred is nothing but sustained anger. . . . The spirit has already declared that . . . "whoever is angry with his brother is liable to judgment; whoever says 'Raca' is liable to the counsil; whoever says 'You fool' is liable to the hell of fire" (Matthew 5:22). (*Institutes*, 8.39; 404)

Thus the fifth commandment drives us to consider a wide range of relationships, to consider all the conditions whereby even we might be peaceable people, to demand of our churches that they enable us to be people who can live together without resorting to violence.

This commandment reminds us that the community of faith (church and Israel) is not only constituted by these commandments but is also the rationale for them. That is, without the community that can produce nonviolence and model and support nonviolent life, these commands seem odd, heroic, or idealistic. They presuppose a community strong enough in its life together, a community that knows how to make peace with one another, to deal with one another in peaceful ways, in order to make these commandments "work." Conflicts will occur. The church is not called to be a place without conflict, but rather a people to whom have been given the means of confession and reconciliation, confrontation and forgiveness, whereby we are able to deal with conflicts without the conventional violence of the world.

William Placher notes how curious it is that the church lives with four Gospels. One might have thought, at some early point, the church would settle down with one authoritative Gospel, would have attempted to harmonize all of the Gospels into one. Why not? Placher surmises that we have Matthew, Mark, Luke, and John because the church practices nonviolence. The only way to achieve unity would be to do violence to someone's voice, to exclude or to coerce artificial unity. So the church's peaceful life together produces a wonderfully rich and diverse community, not because the church affirms some limp value like diversity or inclusiveness, but rather because the church practices nonviolence.[3]

In a sermon on the commandments, Calvin asked why, if God calls us to be perfect, a commandment says that we should not be angry and not murder. Calvin answered that God prohibited killing because, in the Decalogue,

> God spoke in a gross and uncultured manner in order to accommodate himself to the great and the small and the less intelligent. For we know that everyone excuses himself on the grounds of ignorance, and if something appears too obscure and difficult, it seems to us that when we fail we can wash our hands of it if [only] we can say: "that was too lofty and profound for me; I didn't understand it well at all." Therefore in order that men might no longer have [recourse] to such subterfuges, God willed to speak in such a way that little children could understand what he says. This is why, in sum, he says: *"You shall not be murderers."* (*Sermons*, 25)

What Calvin says of the fifth commandment might be said of all. The Decalogue is wonderfully simple, terse, without much qualification or equivocation. As Luther said, when God speaks to us in the commandments, God speaks "baby talk." In a commandment like this one, we can be glad that God deals with us in a "gross and uncultured manner," that God accommodates to "the small and the less intelligent."

It would be wonderful if we could be peaceable in all our dealings with one another. Yet knowing our weakness and simple-mindedness, God just commands us not to kill. In order not to kill, we must eventually acquire the virtues of patience and courage, but for now, just for starters, God tells us not to kill.

One of us has on our door a poster from the Mennonites, saying, "If the Christians of the world would agree not to kill other Christians. . . ." Many, seeing the poster, think it is ridiculous. Why should Christians agree only not to kill other Christians? We shouldn't kill anyone, Christian or otherwise. Right?

In defense of the poster, we say that in a society like ours, if you want peace, you have to begin somewhere and agreeing not to kill other Christians is a radical enough idea for Americans. That is why the Mennonites were right to call their poster, "A Modest Proposal for Peace." In the present administration, it is almost inconceivable that we should be a nation who would not kill Muslims so, if we could just decide that America should never kill Christians, that would be a good start.

Calvin recognized that not killing, one of the simplest and briefest of commandments, requires a whole range of virtues and dispositions, few of which are simple or easy. He counseled,

> Let us learn to look to God in order to obtain a right and pure explanation of the law. Who is the one who is speaking? He who rules over our hearts and our thoughts! He cannot be worshipped by our glance and is not content with our abstaining from evil in our own eyes, rather he wants to be worshipped in spirit and in truth. He wills for our conscience to be pure and chaste, for us to be purged of all malice.
>
> That being true, if we only keep the nature of God in mind, it is no longer necessary to confine the law of God to external works, but it is fitting to conclude that when God speaks of murderers he equally speaks of all enmity, of all indignation and anger, and of all rancor that we harbor against our fellowman. In fact, that is the precise reason why Saint John says that "whoever hates his brother in his heart is [already] a murderer" (1 John 3:15). (*Sermons,* 159)

Learning how not to do what comes naturally (i.e., murder), we learn how vulnerable we are, how dependent we are upon one another. If we are going to be nonviolent, we will need more than a little help from our friends. We will need them in fact to be not only our friends, but also friends with God. Such friends are called "church."

Understood in this way, the fifth commandment calls into question violence-producing activities like our acquisitiveness and accumulation of riches. To be wealthy tends to give one the illusion that we have bought protection, which usually means isolation, so there is little need to cooperate with our fellows. Hunkered down behind our gated communities with their security guards and alarm systems, we don't need to worry about the violence on the streets of less well-heeled neighborhoods.

Accordingly we fail to see the violence in our wealth. We think we are at peace, protected in our safe enclave. Violence is "out there" in the unsafe streets of the inner city. We cannot see that our safety has been bought at the expense of others. We cannot see that the violence of the city, which too often is self-destructive, is a judgment on us. But the fifth commandment is unambiguous—there is a connection between our wealth and the failure to acknowledge the violence called order that we have come to call "peace."

It is only against a background of interpreting the fifth commandment as demanding a peaceful community like the church that we can understand the Christian prohibition against such violent acts as abortion, suicide, and euthanasia. We ought to order our lives together in such a way that these matters simply do not occur among us. We ought to live with and love one another in such a way that none of us are ever so alone that suicide seems a possibility. We ought to so honor and care for our elders that euthanasia seems irrelevant. We ought never to have sex (as we shall see in the next commandment) in a manner that a life conceived through that sex should tempt us to end life. Descriptions like suicide, abortion, euthanasia, words not in the Bible, are descriptions meant to help extend our understanding of how God would have us reverence life. So not ending our lives when we are miserable, not taking the lives of those who are old and infirm, not ending the life of a fetus who has not yet even been born are actions that make no sense, and ought not to make sense, if God does not exist and if it is untrue that our lives are not our own creations.

There is, therefore, a kind of perverted logic to the Religious Right's assertion that (as Dostoyevsky said) without God, everything is permitted. The perversion in their logic is that in defending God in the name of making our social order "moral," what they care most about is the social order. They confuse America with church. They seize upon the Ten Commandments as a universal, general code of conduct for every thinking American and forget how exceptional the community is rendered by the Decalogue. That our society is so terribly violent is in great part the result of the church's failure to be a community of nonviolence as a by-product of our worship of the God of peace. What the Religious Right does not see is that the failure is not out there among those godless secularists, but is rather in here in the church's failure to understand how our wealth leads us to kill in the name of God. You begin by building a nice church, then you establish the clergy pension fund, and the next thing you know you have written a prayer for Colin Powell to pray with the troops on their way to destroy Iraq.

One reason why we Christians argue so much about which hymn to sing, which liturgy to follow, which way to worship is that the commandments teach us to believe that bad liturgy eventually leads to bad ethics. You begin by singing some sappy sentimental hymn, then you pray some pointless prayer, and the next thing you know you have murdered your best friend.

We know a young man who, as a college student, came to his campus minister, saying that if the then-active war on Iraq continued, and if he were drafted, he did not think he could serve. When asked why, he said, "Because I'm studying biology. In biology we tend to love life, to study it, attempt to understand it. I'm on the side of life, not death. Furthermore, I'm a Christian."

That he was a Christian seemed not to extensively inform his incipient pacifism. He had received little instruction in nonviolence from his church. So he decided to meet with his pastor, to tell his hometown pastor that he could not register or participate if there were a draft.

"That's not the position of our denomination," his pastor told him. "Pacifism is idealistic and unrealistic. What would you do if someone was raping your wife? Would you not defend her?" So went his pastor's response.

The student persisted. He realized that this was the first time in his life he had ever swum against the stream, had ever done something contrary to his parents' wishes, had ever resisted the status quo. He therefore enrolled in a campus Bible study group. He asked people to pray for him. Encountering resistance from some of his friends, he discovered new friends who could help him articulate his pacifist resistance and stand by him in case he had to break the law. He began attending church more regularly.

He stopped having sex with the woman he had been dating, realizing that there was some sort of connection between his promiscuity and his acquiescence in a questionable and potentially violent campus culture.

Later he would say, "The best way to become nonviolent is just to have the guts to announce that you are. After that, it's easy. You can't do it by yourself. Those who despise pacifism make you defend your position and, in defending yourself to them, you become more convinced yourself. Those who believe in it become your new friends and reassure you that you don't have to do any of this by yourself. Now, thanks to them, I'm peaceful, more peaceful than I would have been if I had not told people I was a pacifist."

By now you are objecting, "But isn't there a great deal of war in the Old Testament?"

We cannot deal with every passage in the Old Testament about war and killing. Most of the killing in the Old Testament is not celebrated as good, but rather it is presented as a concession to our sin. As for killing in the New Testament, it is exclusively done to Christians, rather than by them, and nowhere is such killing, even if lawfully state-imposed (which most of it is), seen as positive. For now we can only make the point that God, the giver and owner of life, is the only One with the right to take life. The fundamental presumption in Scripture is quite simple—life belongs to God. Life is not an end in itself. Nowhere in the Bible is life spoken of as inherently sacred. Life is God's creation. We stand in awe of life as we stand in awe of God. In this world, there is much worth dying for, as the martyrs remind us, so life can never be an end in itself. By our very nature, life is always slipping away from us, reminding us of our vulnerability, and the blessed giftedness of our lives.

Nowhere in Christian tradition is war simply accepted as a given, nor is there a general justification for war even in the name of defending ourselves. Nor does Christian tradition give justification even for wars in defense of democracies. The claim that democracies are less violent than nondemocracies is simply false. Recent history has shown that democracies are as murderous against their enemies as nondemocracies.

The Christian tradition of war has shaped what many call the just-war tradition. The just-war tradition assumes that those who have authority to take life must do so in the name of controlling or limiting the violence inherent among humans. The decision to enter into a just war must be made only by proper authorities with proper reluctance and without anger or pride. Moreover the war must be fought with just means, which means noncombatants can never be attacked directly. We write as a pacifist and as one attempting to be pacifist, who deny even to the state the right to take life. We are therefore more than willing to join cause with defenders of the just-war tradition, who attempt to put severe limits upon contemporary war's lack of limits. We suspect, however, such an endeavor can be self-deceptive, because those who defend limited use of violence seldom ask how they would know when violence was no longer limited.

Luther, who we believe gave quite unjustified justification for public authorities to kill, joined with Aquinas and Calvin in agreeing that we are murderers when we fail to observe, "I was hungry and thirsty and you gave me no food or drink. I was a stranger, and you did not welcome me; I was naked and you did not clothe me; I was sick and in prison and you did not visit me" (Matthew 25).

Luther said that when we do not visit those in prison we become like the murdering horde. While he did give to civil authorities the right to punish, in place of parents, he wanted that right severely limited. Those who take a life as public officials always bear the burden of proof. Calvin said that those who take life, even in the most just of wars, are soiled. "And why is that? It's important for us to realize that God has created us to live peaceably with each other and that we cannot equip ourselves without this becoming a spot on us and without our already being polluted before God" (*Sermons,* 156). Thus in the Middle Ages, those who had participated in a just war were required, at the war's end, not to march through the streets proud and victorious, but rather to fall to their knees in penance and confession before they could partake of the Eucharist.

Asking people like us (one of us from Texas, the other from South Carolina) not to kill is utterly nonsensical—if we are not people of God. Believing us to be God's people, the commandments are so bold as to demand that we not kill. In so doing, demand is transformed into gift, into good news of our redemption. Acting as if we were peaceful, as if God's promises were true, we become peaceable people. God uses our fidelity as a means of carving out a little piece of enemy territory for the Kingdom.

Is it any wonder that Israel thought the law to be a great gift?

Notes

1. As quoted in *Time,* July 6, 1998, 36.
2. Ibid., 38.
3. William Placher, *Unapologetic Theology: A Christian in a Pluralistic Conversation* (Westminster/John Knox Press, 1989), 125.

Chapter Six

> *You shall not commit adultery.*
> —Exodus 20:14

The Sixth Commandment

Judge Roy Moore of Etowah County, Alabama, was sued by the ACLU and the Alabama Free Thought Association in 1995 for displaying the Ten Commandments on his courtroom wall. A Montgomery County judge ruled that Moore must take the commandments down from his wall. The Alabama Supreme Court issued a stay, but Governor Fob James promised to call out the National Guard to protect Judge Moore and the Ten Commandments from the federal courts.

One of our Alabama relatives said, "Don't worry about anybody in the state legislature wanting to hang the Ten Commandments in the legislative chamber. Until they can figure out a way to do something about that thing on adultery, the senators want to keep those commandments in court and as far away from themselves as possible."

Luther said that, from the previous commandment prohibiting murder, we were to learn how to live next door to our neighbor. In this commandment we learn how to live with the neighbor who lies next to us in bed. Indeed, Aquinas, noting that in the marriage service we call the wife and husband "one flesh," related the prohibition against adultery to the prohibition against murder since the two are one body.

The Reformers expanded this commandment as applying not simply to marital infidelity but to all forms of unchastity and fornication. Why? In fornication the man is not sinning against one to whom he is married but is having sex with someone to whom he is not married. So how can fornication be called adultery? Aquinas said the "one body" talk of marriage is a reflection of baptism since, in baptism, both man and woman are related to the body, the Body of Christ.

Aquinas admitted that the explanation of the sixth commandment to include fornication is curious. However, he reasoned,

> One might say there is no reason why fornication should be a mortal sin, since the body of the wife is not given, as in adultery. I say, however, if the body of the wife is not given, nevertheless, there is given the Body of Christ which was given to the husband when he was sanctified in Baptism. If, then, one must not betray his wife, with much more reason must he not be unfaithful to Christ: "Know you not that your bodies are the members of Christ? Shall I then take the members of Christ and make them the members of a harlot? God forbid!" (1 Corinthians 6:15). (*The Catechetical Instructions,* 102)

Like Aquinas, Luther and Calvin also maintained that the commandment against adultery not only forbids adultery, but every form of immodesty and impurity. What once was thought to be for the married has now become wonderfully egalitarian. Christians are called to chastity, whether married or not. Not only the external act is forbidden but, according to Luther, every kind of cause, motive, and means:

> Your heart, your lips, and your whole body are to be chaste and to afford no occasion, aid, or encouragement to unchastity. Moreover, you are to defend, protect, and rescue your neighbor whenever he is in danger or need, and on the contrary to aid and assist him so that he may retain his honor. Whenever you fail to do this (though you could prevent a wrong) or wink at it as if it were no concern of yours, you are just as guilty as the culprit himself. In short, everyone is required both to live chastely himself and to

help his neighbor do the same. Thus God by his commandment wants every husband or every wife guarded and protected from any trespass. (*The Large Catechism*, 36-37)

Now all this may seem to some to be making a great deal of fuss over the body. Presumably, there may be gods who have little interest in how bodies are used or abused since these gods are mainly concerned with spiritual matters. The God of Israel and the church, however, is clearly opinionated about bodies and bodily, carnal acts, our pots and pans and genitals. All Christian theologians read the sixth commandment through the lens of Matthew 5:27-28, "You have heard that it was said, 'You shall not commit adultery.' But I say to you that everyone who looks at a woman with lust has already committed adultery with her in his heart."

Calvin noted that we tend toward deceit, especially when it comes to sexual matters. Thus lust is prohibited by Christ so that no one might think it possible to be innocently lustful. There is always the danger of adultery. Just as Calvin, in his comments on the previous commandment, noted the connection between anger and murder, so here he again connects emotional dispositions with actions. Furthermore, Calvin draws us to a consideration of the connection between deceit and sexual sin, lying and adultery. In few areas of human endeavor are we more deceitful than in sex. "I love you," as ethicist Paul Ramsey noted, too often means "I love me and want to use you." So we do well to test our declarations of love by the promises of marriage for evidence of self-deceit.

In his discussion of intercourse, Calvin turns not to further consideration of human nature, anthropology—the move contemporary theologians usually make—but rather toward theology. This commandment, Calvin said, drives us to

continually return to the nature of God, realizing that he is not an earthly lawgiver who only forbids the external act while permitting us to indulge evil affections, for God has no desire to be served with the eye, nor is he like us. Men are satisfied when they cannot perceive their faults, but God who fathoms our hearts sees the truth, as Jeremiah explains. He not merely wanted to restrain our bodies in his law, but above all he considered our souls. Consequently let us note that God has not simply forbidden the act that would in effect violate marriage or break it, but he has forbidden all lasciviousness and wicked intentions. And that is why our Lord Jesus Christ says that when a man looks upon another man's wife with lust, he is an adulterer in God's eyes. Although he is not guilty according to human laws and cannot be chastised for having acted promiscuously, nevertheless in God's sight he is already condemned as having transgressed this commandment here. (*Sermons,* 171)

Once again we are given a commandment that presupposes the virtues related to the worship of a true God, membership in a community of virtue whereby we are given the resources not natural to ourselves, whereby we are enabled to live in peace with one another. As we have noted, learning to live in peace involves learning to name our lives as gifts, to receive new life as a gift. For instance, there is no way to separate our ethics of abortion from the way we live our lives sexually. We cannot give a wink about promiscuity and at the same time vigorously prohibit abortion. If abortion is wrong and ought to be prohibited among Christians, that presupposes a community whereby we are given the resources not to commit the violence that abortion names. Marriage is therefore seen by us as a gift that expands our lives, training us to be ready to receive children, even as we have received one another in marriage. Marriage, its promises, and the manner of life it entails, are the God-given means to avoid the self-deceit and violence that seem inherent to sex without promise.

After noting how highly God must honor and glorify married life by God's insertion of adultery into the Decalogue, Luther said that it is significant that God, "established [marriage] as the first of all institutions, and he created man and woman differently (as is evident) not for lewdness but to be true to each other, be fruitful, beget children, and support and bring them up to the glory of God' " (*The Large Catechism,* 37).

The Sixth Commandment in Christian Life

The God of Israel and the church is a faithful God. Time and again in the history of God's people, God has been faithful to us even when our love failed and we were unfaithful. In this commandment, men and women in marriage have the opportunity to mirror in our little lives and relationships some of the fidelity that God has shown to us. The skills, understandings, confession, and forgiveness required of men and women to be faithful in marriage are analogous to how we learned to respond to God's faithfulness to the church.

Frequently in the Old Testament, idolatry is spoken of in terms of adultery. As we have said, this relationship between us and God is emotionally charged, personal. Sex is rightly regarded with how we live with God and vice versa. Sin against a spouse is also sin against God's intentions for how women and men are to live.

In pushing sex out into public view, the Ten Commandments are making some rather astounding claims about sex. We have been conditioned to think of sex as personal, private. But here, sex goes public. Somehow the whole future of Israel as God's people is tied to how it goes for us as women and men.

The prohibition against adultery applies both to those in marriage and those who are betrothed to be married (cf. Leviticus 18:6-20; 20:10-21). Admittedly, there is a double standard at work here, for men are said to commit adultery only with other married women while women are said to commit adultery if they have sex with any man, married or otherwise. Of course, Jesus elaborated and expanded the sixth commandment, in the ways we have noted, so Christians have no choice but to apply the prohibition against adultery to men as well as women.

What does it mean for the commandments to take sex so seriously, to deny sex the casual, desacralized status it has for many within a culture that speaks of sex as "scoring," "hitting," "hooking up"? The Bible knows nothing of our current notion of sexuality as some independently intelligible human characteristic. Sexuality, as we have been taught by modernity to conceive it, was the creation of the presumption that unless someone is fulfilled sexually (and the only way that can happen, as far as modernity is concerned, is through sexual activity) then somehow that person is less than a person. To deny someone's sexual expression is to deny the highest of that person's humanity. So the world goes through laborious labeling of people as "straight," "gay," "bisexual," "transgendered," in its rather pitiful attempts to make sexuality independently significant, to exalt sex as the most interesting, most determinative aspect of human beings. One reason why we have become such a sex-saturated society is that capitalism, having rendered sex into a commodity, discovered a good fit between the consumptive aspects of sex and advertising. Sex features so prominently in the world of Madison Avenue because the fulfillment of desire has become the distinguishing mark of humanity, a humanity now routinely referred to, in a rare moment of modern honesty, simply as "consumers."

In such a climate, Christians need to be reminded that for us, we are called not to marry or to have children but first to be single, even some to lifelong celibacy. The church grows and lives by witness and conversion, not by marriage and family. Sex is not the most interesting activity Christians can perform. After all, even dogs do it with no instruction. We have children not because the church needs natural regeneration, the siring of offspring, but rather we have children so that we might witness to them, so that fathers and mothers might assume the office of evangelist in their instruction to their children. Those who are single in the church also bear parental responsibilities since, in baptism, everyone in the church is a parent. As Sunday school teachers, confirmation mentors, and faithful examples of the faith, single people can do much to nurture our children in the faith. Part of the vocation of single people who care for children through the church is living lives of sexual responsibility, which show that they can be trusted with the church's children in all circumstances.

Because Christians do not have to marry to be faithful to Christ, marriage is viewed by us as a calling to be tested by the church. It is not the single who must explain their status to the church but the married. The modern notion that simply because two people love each other and need each other they should be married is not a Christian idea. The only good Christian reason to get married is the conviction that you can live out your baptismal vocation better within marriage than without.

Furthermore, we believe that love is the fruit of marriage, the result of our faithful commitment to one another rather than its cause. At the service of marriage, the pastor does not say,

"Donna, do you love Don?" Rather the question is, "Donna, *will* you love Don?" Love is here defined as something one decides to do, a future fruit of marriage rather than the cause of marriage, a promise, a vocation of some, but not all. Love is not a feeling, but a commitment, a promise, a gift one makes to God and to another person in gratitude for the gifts given to us by God and others.

More specifically, for Christians marriage is justified for the upbuilding of the community, not for the mutual pleasure of the couple. We do believe that marriage can be pleasurable, joyful, but the pleasure and joy begin not in private concerns but in public commitments. The pleasure of sex is enhanced by doing it in public, that is, in enjoying sexuality within the context of our wider Christian ministry, our openness to new life and to children. Thus we discover the joy of the primal act of being "fruitful," of participating in the very creativity of God as God intended.

The Catechism of the Catholic Church speaks of chastity as a basic virtue for both those who are married and those who are single because, in chastity, a Christian "maintains the integrity of the powers of life and love" placed in us, which ensures "the unity of the person; is opposed to any behavior that would impair it, and tolerates neither a double life nor duplicity of speech." Lots of lying seems to be required for the practice of adultery, the living of a double life. So the Catholics say in the *Catechism* that "chastity includes an apprenticeship in self-mastery which is a training for freedom" (p. 562).

Note that the *Catechism* links fidelity in marriage to truthfulness. The covenant of marriage provides the opportunity for honest speech. When a relationship is thought to be fragile, lying seems necessary to sustain it. When our conversation as men and women is upheld by the promises of marriage, we can risk telling the truth to one another, which is one reason why many experience marriage as liberating rather than restricting, because it may be their first experience of being truthful with another human being in a society full of lies. Thereby marriage becomes a context within the church, where we receive training in the truthfulness that ought to characterize the speech of all the baptized.

Thus fidelity is experienced by Christians not so much as a burden but as the blessing of discovering that we are made better persons in this relationship than we could have been without the promises of marriage. We are given the opportunity to be truthful. The longer we try to keep the promises of marriage, the less we have to try. We become as we have professed. We can be trusted, even with a matter so explosive and potentially untrustworthy as sex. That we can be so happy in marriage, despite what we thought were our natural inclinations, is an indication that God has created us for fidelity. In keeping our promises, in being faithful to our commitments, we can look back on our lives with joy that, because of our promises, God has enabled us to make our lives *our* lives. You have never had good sex until you have had it with a Christian.

You already know the objections to this sort of reasoning. It goes something like, "There's nothing wrong with sex outside of marriage as long as the people involved understand why they are doing it and as long as nobody gets hurt." This assumes that in order to be hurt you have to know that you are being hurt. Part of the hurt of our sexual sin is that the hurt is not often known until much later, when we come to regret some past act. Furthermore, whether we think it hurts or not, sin injures our ability to lead truthful lives for the upbuilding of the community.

One of the ways the church has attempted to talk about marriage is by saying that marriage has both a unitive and a procreative end. If two people do not have children, it does not mean that their marriage is less than a marriage. It means that they have together fulfilled the unitive purpose of marriage. Of course that they do not have biological children does not mean, at least as far as the church is concerned, they are free from parental tasks. Indeed we believe everyone in the church has parental responsibilities derived from our baptism.

The procreative end of marriage is the way the church has maintained that one of the essential gifts of marriage is children. The term "planned parenthood" doesn't quite fit how Christians ought to have children, for children are not our choice as much as they are God's choice of us. Much harm has been done to children in our era through children being reduced to projects of the parents. Children are not our achievements, or our rights, or our projects. They are God's gifts. Of course, the gift of children is sometimes a gift that disrupts our lives, creating all sorts of anarchy. Sometimes our dull little lives need the gift of some divine anarchy. Christians know that our lives are not meant merely to be safe, therefore God gives us something more interesting to do with our lives than maintaining mere security. God gives us children.

Moreover, children pull us into time, demanding that we make time to enjoy the sheer wonder of their lives in a world that too often denies children simply because, having become gods unto ourselves, we are too busy. The same God who created time, who entered time in the Exodus and in the resurrection of Jesus, is determined for us to redeem our time, to pass our time in important matters like caring for children, to witness to the world that, despite the uncertainties and terrors of tomorrow, God has given us the means to live into the future by giving birth to and raising children. One of the most moving testimonials to faith in God was the willingness of Jews to have children, even in the days of the Holocaust. Our openness to children is a witness to our faith that God, not nations, rules the world and writes the future.

We hope that we have not spoken of sex in too instrumental and less pleasurable a way. Sex was created by God from the first, in Genesis, and is to be thoroughly enjoyed. Yet sex has been disordered by sin. That sin is not lust, though lust can be a symptom of our disorder. Lust can be part of our violent manipulation of one another in the perversion of love and intimacy. In the abuse of women, in the failure of men to take responsibility for their children, we see the results of our disordered sex. That is why the church particularly condemned so-called secret marriage. That is, a private arrangement between two people. In contrast the church insisted upon sex going public, that is, in sex only within the public acknowledgment of commitment, "before God and these witnesses" as the traditional service of marriage puts it.

There are varieties of ways to be married, depending upon cultural and class divisions, depending upon the unique differences between a man and a woman in marriage. Different things can be

expected of men and women in marriage. Yet none of this justi-
fies deviation from the sixth commandment. Christians who are
called to marriage are called to practice lifetime, exclusive,
monogamous fidelity. Christians who remain single are called to
support marriage. Any debate about divorce or remarriage after
divorce must take place against the background of this command
and the community it envisions. In mainline Protestantism, we
have not really debated divorce and remarriage against the background of our beliefs about God, other than a sentimental notion
of "grace." What we have done is simply to leave such decisions
to the private consciences of people, and as a result we have
abandoned people to their own self-deceit or to enslavement by
a consumerist culture.

Yes, marriage can be a hellish nightmare of manipulation and
violence. Marriage, like nonviolence, is too difficult to practice
alone, too prone to perversion when done outside a judging, forgiving, witnessing community. Some marriages today are miserable not because people are not committed to marriage, but
because that is their only commitment. Marriage is symbiotic, it
lives off of and derives power from our other commitments.
When marriage is constricted to a relationship between two people, rather than a practice of the whole church, marriage tends to
collapse under its own weight.

Marriage alone, the relationship of two detached individuals
clinging to one another, isolated from some larger good other than
the emotional or economic enhancement of the two individuals, is
doomed to collapse. Marriage standing alone, for all its virtues,
simply cannot lift the luggage. Therefore, in thinking about marriage we first think about the church and our vocation to serve
Christ, then we move to consideration of how marriage might
enhance that vocation. Christians believe that when practiced
within the church, marriage liberates us from our own arbitrary
desire and gives us something good to do on ordinary days, which
are most days, with ordinary people, which means most of us. The
sixth commandment thus becomes not some impossible demand,
but a gracious invitation to ordinary people to become rather
extraordinary saints who are known for their lifetimes of fidelity.

It is at once frightening and wonderful that we now live in a world that is so morally chaotic that a mundane matter like taking some care with whom we have sex renders us into heroes.

Some time ago one of us met a young man at a conference on evangelism in the Episcopal Church. After my speech, we walked around the lake at the conference center. He said to me, "I don't think we Episcopalians are going to be very evangelical. It's just not in our nature to be too pushy. We keep our religion to ourselves."

"You certainly do," I agreed.

Then he told me about a young woman he had met in California. They were on their first date. It went well. Their conversation was scintillating; they really seemed to be working well together. Then, toward the end of the evening, she said, "Well, do you want to go to your place or mine? I've got a big day tomorrow."

"What are you talking about?" he asked.

"You know," she said. "Don't you find me attractive?"

"Of course," he said. "But this is our first date! I hardly know you. We can't sleep together."

"But I always sleep with guys on the first date," she replied.

"I don't do that!" he said.

"But why don't you?" she asked.

"Because . . . I'm an Episcopalian," he answered. "We're funny about who we sleep with."

"Episcopalian. What's that?" she asked.

"Well, it's a kind of Christian," he replied.

He then told her about his church. She was fascinated, had never heard such a thing. So he invited her to visit with him the next Sunday. She did. "She thought it was the greatest thing she ever saw. Three weeks later, she asked our priest to baptize her. She now thinks she invented the Episcopal Church, even though we're not dating anymore."

These days, just one person running loose in southern California who keeps the sixth commandment is enough to attract a crowd. Call it ordinary folk like us getting to be saints.

Chapter Seven

> *You shall not steal.*
> —Exodus 20:15

The Seventh Commandment

In the middle of instruction to the saints at Ephesus, the writer says, "Thieves must give up stealing; rather let them labor and work honestly with their own hands, so as to have something to share with the needy" (Ephesians 4:28). Thieves in church? The rationale for honest labor rather than thievery is refreshing. It is not because property is private, but rather so as "to have something to share with the needy." Perhaps even more refreshing is a church whose evangelism is more than simply gathering "people like us," but rather it is so interesting that even thieves are attracted to it. More interesting is an early Christian preacher who knew that in your average congregation, thievery is probably present. These days, from a Christian point of view, it is quite an accomplishment to know when one is a thief.

According to Aquinas,

"Thou shalt not kill" forbids us to injure our neighbor in his own person; "Thou shall not commit adultery" forbids injury to the person to whom one is bound in marriage; and now the Commandment, "Thou shalt not steal," forbids us to injure our neighbor in his goods. This Commandment forbids any worldly goods whatsoever to be taken away wrongfully. (*The Catechetical Instructions,* 105)

In our present circumstances the difficulty with this commandment is that we are unsure what worldly goods are ours and what
goods are our neighbor's and what it means for them to be taken
wrongly. Christian tradition has assumed, given that we are creatures who live in a good creation, that whatever is "ours" is so
only as gift, grace. Therefore goods are rightly seen as first of all
goods that are in common. Any possession we may have is possession that is in service to wider good. As we sometimes sing in
church at the offering,

> *We give Thee but Thine own,*
> *Whate'er the gift may be;*
> *All that we have is Thine alone,*
> *A trust, O Lord, from Thee.*

Thus for Aquinas theft can involve not paying wages that are due.
A theft is any fraud in buying or selling. Theft is committed if anyone buys promotions to positions of temporal or spiritual honor,
such as those who spend money campaigning for bishop.

Luther may even be more forceful than Aquinas in this matter,
arguing that stealing is nothing less than acquiring any property
by any unjust means. Luther begins with the assumption that the
world is a system of thievery in which, of all the sins that possess us, thievery is the most common craft on earth. "If we look
at mankind in all its conditions, it is nothing but a vast, wide sta-
ble full of great thieves" (*The Large Catechism,* 40). Luther
observed further that, "Stealing is a widespread, common vice,
but people pay so little attention to it that the matter is entirely
out of hand. If all who are thieves, though they are unwilling to
admit it, were hanged on the gallows, the world would soon be
empty, and there would be a shortage of both hangmen and gallows" (p. 39).

Luther could make these quite startling claims because like
Aquinas, he assumed that a person steals not only when he robs
a person's strongbox or picks a pocket, but when "he takes
advantage of his neighbor at the market, in a grocery shop,
butcher stall, wine and beer cellar, workshop, and in short, whenever business is transacted and money is exchanged for goods or

labor." Luther would not have been surprised by Karl Marx's analysis of capitalism as a system of legalized theft.

Given the desires that shape our lives, we moderns are more likely to view the commandment against adultery as the most onerous. That is a mistake. The most difficult commandments for us are these dealing with stealing and lying because they cut to the heart of the deceit upon which our lives are built. We simply do not want to acknowledge that we are caught up in systems that make it impossible to discover how deeply implicated we are in theft and lying. Just as lies are parasitic on the truth and known only by the willingness of some to speak the truth, so theft can be known only when there is an alternative to the presumption, upon which, according to many interests, the U.S. Constitution is based, namely, that we are essentially self-seeking, self-interested creatures who will survive only if we get "ours." The church has failed in its responsibility to evangelize and to witness to a democratic, constitutionally formed world of self-interest that there is hell to pay for breaking the seventh commandment. The church has not presented the world with a clear institutional, socially embodied alternative to Toys R Us and Amway.

Aquinas made no concessions in this respect. For him the gravity of theft is nothing less than murder. Quoting Ecclesiastes 34:25 and 27, he notes, "The bread of the needy is the life of the poor; he that defraudeth them therefore is a man of blood." Again, "He that sheddeth blood and he that defraudeth the laborer of his hire are brothers" (*The Catechetical Instructions,* 106).

Calvin echoes the association by Aquinas of theft with murder, as the former notes that too often the rich, under the guise of their authority, wrong their neighbor who is poor and thus become thieves and murderers. Calvin asserts that such actions do not simply constitute theft, but in fact stealing from the neighbor is equivalent to murder. Calvin observes that this crime is made worse because often the thief is applauded. Indeed he is not just applauded, but honored because he is such a big thief. For, as a man's estate grows, people woo him and he becomes more admired. Therefore, as far as the world is concerned, quite often it is through theft that people are honored.

But Calvin said we should not let the honoring of thieves blind us. The scripture is clear that there will always be thieves among us. Given their existence, how are we able to know what theft is? Calvin suggests that, if we really want to know what stealing is, we must consider what doing the right thing for our neighbor would be. "Now we do not do our neighbors justice when we rob them of their goods, or, by whatever means is available, add to ourselves what is theirs. For, in brief, whenever we employ any malice or outrage[ous means], we are sufficiently refuted" (*Sermons*, 190).

Calvin's observation that to know what constitutes theft requires a positive alternative is surely right. One way such an alternative has been named in the past is in the language of the common good. Such a good is not just the sum of individual interests, but rather a good that is genuinely common just to the extent it cannot exist separate from the practices that constituted the community. Parks constitute the common good, as do art and community shelters. The peculiar pathology of our time is to make private what should be common.

The difficulty, of course, is that most of us who are rich did not "try" to be rich. We were just lucky. But we think it important to believe we somehow deserved our wealth. The idea that we might be rich because we benefited from a system that is built on theft is unthinkable. How could we acknowledge that this might be the case and continue to live in the manner to which we have become accustomed? We cannot. We cannot see how our wealth is hurting us.

The rich are insatiable and can never be content. Having much, they fear the loss of what they have and think the only way to protect what they have is to have more. They thus are tormented and unable to enjoy what they have. Calvin did not need a contemporary psychologist's theory of the "rising threshold of expectation" (the more we have, the more we want) to explain the misery of the miser. Wealth turns out to be just another name for loneliness. The rich, in short, simply cannot learn to rest easy in God's good creation.

When Jesus was questioned about inheritance (Luke 12:13-21), he told the story of the rich fool, the rich man who attempted to secure his life through large barns. In that parable, the rich man's speech is all monologue, soliloquy—"I know what I will do. I will pull down my barns and build larger ones, I will say, 'Soul, take ease,' I . . ." The rich tend to talk a great deal to themselves, having little need, in their wealth, to be in conversation with others about the larger good. Wealth and loneliness tend to go together, it would appear.

Furthermore, the rich man says to himself, "Soul . . . take your ease" (Luke 12:19 RSV). Yet ease is precisely what the rich cannot take, for they are caught on a treadmill of constantly expanding demanding desire.

Therefore they break not only the seventh commandment but also the third. They know no Sabbath. Luther observed that the rich may disregard this commandment, but they will not escape God's wrath and punishment. Though the rich may be defiant and arrogant, safely insulated by their riches from life's vicissitudes, finally they will have to see what they have gained. They will ultimately be judged by God.

> Let them keep on boldly fleecing people as long as they can. God will not forget his commandment. He will pay them what they deserve. . . . Daily they leave the poor defrauded. New burdens and high prices are imposed. Everyone misuses the market in his own willful, conceited, arrogant way, as if it were his right and privilege to sell his goods as dearly as he pleased without a word of criticism. We shall stand by and let such persons fleece, grab, and hoard. But we shall trust God, who takes matters into his own hands. After they have scrimped and scraped for a long time, he will pronounce this kind of blessing over them: "Your grain will spoil in the garner and your beer in the cellar. Your cattle will die in the stall. Yes, where you have cheated and defrauded anyone out of a gulden, your entire hoard will be consumed by rust so that you will never enjoy it." (*The Large Catechism,* 41)

A generation ago, Rudyard Kipling gave an address to the graduating medical class of McGill University, saying, "You will go out of here, and very likely you'll make a lot of money. One day you'll meet someone for whom that means very little. Then you will know how poor you are."[1] We are judged by and for our sin.

Being rich, having possessions we do not need, has disastrous results for our children. For if the ruin of wealth does not work its way out from those who first desire it, there is no question it takes its toll on their children. Sin really is visited upon our children, and their children's children, as the Bible warns. Calvin said,

> Take a father who has pillaged and robbed, who has throughout his life provoked God's vengeance on himself. Is he guilty of murder? Why, he thinks his children ought to be little kings. Now if they were left with only a little with which to set themselves up in business and had to learn to work honestly, his children would have more than enough with which to be satisfied. But insofar as they trust in the goods which have been illegally acquired, their father has set them up for the hangman's noose, or to perish in some horrible way. And why is that? Because the wrath of God consumes all property acquired through graft and robbery. It is even appropriate for such a man's house to be cursed. [For] it is essential for God to reveal himself as a just judge against both thieves and all who scorn his divine majesty. For when you speak to them about this, you only hear the scoffers say: "Well, well, it's time for more money," as it's all the same to them. And when a poor man has neither the strength nor influence to counter them, alas! they bathe in their iniquities. But what? When God sees that these men are that stupid, and that he cannot lead them into a heavenly life, and that it means nothing to them to be excluded from the kingdom of heaven. "Behold," he says, "I have already set the date for your trial. I intend to begin to execute my judgment. I intend to show you that my curse is on illgotten goods and that those who possess them for a [brief] time will of necessity be dispossessed. And both they and their goods will be consumed with all their kind." (*Sermons,* 198-99)

"At MTV we don't shoot for the 14-year-olds, we own them," says MTV Chair Bob Pittman.[2] As Luther said, whatever you would sacrifice your daughter to, that is your god.

It seems too simplistic, amid the analysis of all that is wrong with America, to suggest that what's wrong is that we are rich. Moreover, such riches do not seem to be acquired, at least from our perspective, by theft. We simply assume that because we are rich we deserve to be rich. Since the world is self-created, and what we have is unaccountable to any higher standard than our own conscience, our riches seem to be unquestionably deserved. No theft here. Yet we think that Americans are literally dying (and killing) for our wealth.

In one of our last churches, the foremost family problem was wealth. This might seem strange to say, for the congregation was blue collar, middle class, with no "rich" people. But these people were the first in their families to have a surplus of discretionary funds to spend on their families. Desiring to be "good parents," in the only way they knew, they purchased cars, clothes, and other accoutrements of the "good life" for their children. Spoiled brats were often the unintended result, the production of children who had no resources to say No, indeed who had not the resources even to know there was something worth saying No to. It does not take a huge amount of money to ruin a child. Around us our children are seemingly doing quite well; but what do our riches give us—no children. They become people without hope consumed with consuming to no purpose.

From this perspective, Yuppies can be seen as the monks of modernity. The Yuppies—rich as they are, brought up to believe their task in life is to be richer than their parents, to consume at a higher level than their parents—refrain from having children. Many Yuppies are fated to be Dinks—dual income, no kids. That is their great sacrifice for their gods. The childlessness of the Dinks is not so much a commentary on their selfishness. That they have no purpose for marriage other than themselves is an ascetic discipline since they do not wish to pass on the meaninglessness of their own lives to future generations. Clearly we are dying from our riches. Our misery is testimony to the unmistakable clarity of the reiterated gospel claim that to be rich is to be in big trouble.

The Seventh Commandment in Christian Life

Few in Scripture despise and fear the rich, particularly when they are in the church, more than James:

Come now, you rich people, weep and wail for the miseries that are coming to you. Your riches have rotted, and your clothes are moth-eaten. Your gold and silver have rusted, and their rust will be evidence against you, and it will eat your flesh like fire. You have laid up treasure for the last days. Listen! The wages of the laborers who mowed your fields, which you kept back by fraud, cry out, and the cries of the harvesters have reached the ears of the Lord of hosts. You have lived on the earth in luxury and in pleasure; you have fattened your hearts in a day of slaughter. You have condemned and murdered the righteous one, who does not resist you.

—James 5:1-6

This is the Christian commentary on "You shall not steal."

Of course our defense is, We're not really rich. The really rich are those with millions; whereas we just have thousands. We, moreover, give to this or that charity. We do not think of ourselves as deserving such harsh judgment as James pronounces. We're simply trying to get along.

We take no pleasure in pointing out that we fail to tell ourselves the truth about our wealth. There is every reason to want to hide the truth from ourselves. Lying and riches seem to work hand in hand. Indeed, to be wealthy is to be encouraged to hide the truth from ourselves. For example, what is more deceptive than the presumption that I really don't want all that I have; I'm just trying to prepare a good life for my children. Or that it is not really wealth itself that is the problem, but our *attitude* toward our wealth. Such strategies are but invitations to deception and therefore damnation. We are told, "Give to him who begs from you, and do not refuse him who would borrow from you" (Matthew 5:42 RSV), and we do not think that could be a policy. But just to the extent that we do not think it always could be enacted in our lives, we become thieves. As St. John Chrysostom declared, "Not to enable the poor to share in our goods is to steal from them and deprive them of life. The goods we possess are not ours but theirs" (*Homily on Lazarus* 2.5).

Surely one of the most challenging aspects to our lives today is the importance of meaningful work. In the absence of meaningful work—that is, work that gives us a sense of genuine service to our neighbor—work simply becomes a means of acquiring status and power. We want to be in positions in which others must attend to us, but we do not need to attend to them. We seek to be honored, taking from others the honor that is due them.

We can offer no easy solutions since we ourselves feel so caught. We know at the very least we must cease telling ourselves lies about our position. Calvin noted that there is more to being a redeemed rich man than simply not wanting to increase his gain, but rather it is imperative for us to be poor in our hearts. By that he means:

> We ought not place any pride or confidence in our riches, or use them as occasions for oppressing the weak and those who have no credit or support, as far as the world is concerned. For in the final analysis, we must be ready to become poor if that should be God's will. Whoever is clearly rich today, who has full caves and granaries, a well-lined purse, fields, possessions, and a full string of merchandise, let him not be surprised if God should will to remove it all; may it not inopportune or chagrin him too much, but may he arrive at Job's patience and be able to say, "May God's name be praised, since it has pleased him to take back what he has given me."
>
> That is why (I say) it is so difficult to know [how] to be rich. For unless we come [to the point where we are willing] to submit to God's will, to receive peaceably all that he gives us, that is to say, to bear our poverty with patience when he sends it to us and to be content with our goods which he has put in our hands without abandoning our hearts to them, of necessity we will always be thieves. (*Sermons,* 194)

Of course, the great trick is to know how to have possessions without "abandoning our hearts to them." We can tell ourselves we are ready to lose all that we have, or at least a good deal of it, but how would we know? Christians have thought the development of the virtues of temperance and justice to be crucial for not being possessed by our possessions. Temperance, that is, the moderate attachment to the world's goods, and the pursuit of justice, limiting our desire to pursue our neighbors' goods as well as increasing our desire to render them what is their due, are the ways we learn to be a people who are not captured by theft. To be able to say, "Enough is enough," to see our neighbor's need as a claim upon our possessions, are great, though difficult, virtues. Such virtues are necessary if we are not to be possessed by the lust for gain that otherwise seizes our lives.

Such virtues are necessary if we are to learn to pray the prayer Jesus taught us without regret. In that prayer we ask to be given our "daily bread." It is enough. It is a great deal to be given our daily bread when so many in the world do not receive even bread on a daily basis. So not to be caught by a world of theft requires prayer. The first attitude of prayer is to receive, not to ask, to listen rather than to speak, to be willing by prayer to be formed rather than to use prayer to inform. Through learning to receive, we may be a people capable of sharing.

The habit of being forced by the church to give a tithe may not be all that is required to be obedient to the seventh commandment, but one must begin somewhere. In teaching us to let go of even 10 percent of our stuff, the church is offering us a habit worth cultivating. Most mainline Protestant church members give only 1 to 2 percent of their income to the church. The church needs to demand more. Gratitude is a great virtue, to be cultivated with enthusiasm by a church caught in a materialistic culture. Obedience may also be a prime virtue, giving to God and neighbor simply because we are ordered to do so. There's a reason why the most bitter, acrimonious fights in church are over money rather than theology.

"What's 'stewardship'?" asked our next-door rabbi.

"It's when the church asks for support for its ministry," we replied.

"Do you mean money?" the rabbi asked.

"Yes, money, but also time and talent," we answered.

"You *ask?* Jews are *told* to give money. If you are a Jew, you give. Simple as that."

Christians need to be reminded that Christians as Christians are commanded to give. We give not from philanthropy (which means literally "love of humanity"), but rather out of love for the God who loved us enough to command us to give.

As Jesus said, our wallet and our heart tend to be located in the same place on our anatomy. Jesus appears to have despised few people, except for his documented loathing of the rich. As he noted, it is tough enough for anybody to be shoved through the eye of a needle and thereby to be saved (Luke 18:25-30). For the rich, clutching all of our stuff, it's impossible.

The good news of the seventh commandment is that through obedience, even the salvation of the rich is possible because, with God, anything is possible, even this.

Awe came upon everyone, because many wonders and signs were being done by the apostles. All who believed were together and had all things in common; they would sell their possessions and goods and distribute the proceeds to all, as any had need. Day by day, as they spent much time together in the temple, they broke bread at home and ate their food with glad and generous hearts, praising God and having the goodwill of all the people. And day by day the Lord added to their number those who were being saved.

—Acts 2:43-47

Few moments in Sunday worship are more moving than when, in the Eucharist, members of the congregation hold out their empty hands to receive the Body of Christ. Their hands are open and empty, their tight grip on their possessions has been released. The church has enabled them to assume a posture of receptivity. Those who have so much appear, with empty hands outstretched, to be those who are hungry, needing the gift of bread and wine. One loaf, when shared in Eucharist, is enough.

In learning to bend our lives in truthful confession of our sin, in receiving our lives as gifts, we are saved.

Notes

1. Quoted in *Leadership,* Fall 1995, 21.
2. In Marva J. Dawn, *Reaching Out Without Dumbing Down* (Grand Rapids: William B. Eerdmans, 1995), 17.

Chapter Eight

> *You shall not bear false witness against your neighbor.*
> —Exodus 20:16

The Eighth Commandment

Calvin put it this way:

> Since God (who is truth) abhors a lie, we must practice truth without deceit toward one another. To sum up, then: let us not malign anyone with slanders or false charges, nor harm his substance by falsehood, in short, injure him by unbridled evilspeaking and imprudence. To this prohibition the command is linked that we should faithfully help everyone as much as we can in affirming the truth, in order to protect the integrity of his name and possessions. (*Institutes* 411)

Everything we have been trying to say in our exposition of the commandments comes to a head with this commandment. Calvin, in his Sermon on the Decalogue, asks why God mentions false testimonies and lying since God has already said that we "shall not take the name of the Lord your God in vain" (*Sermons,* 204). This seems to be superfluous repetition. In so short a summary of the Law, Calvin observed that it does not make sense to reiterate the same thing. Yet Calvin explained the repetition by suggesting that behind the eighth commandment is the assumption that the inability to speak truthfully to one another has everything to do with our inability to speak truthfully of God. So according to Calvin, God gave us this commandment to remind us that, being creatures created to speak truthfully to one another, our lives are distorted when what we say to one another is not disciplined by the worship of a true God.

The very title of this book, *The Truth About God,* is meant to reflect Herbert McCabe's extraordinary observation that it is not so much God who reveals to us the Ten Commandments, but the Ten Commandments that reveal God to us (*What Ethics Is All About,* 57). We have been created for friendship with God and with one another. Nothing is more important for friendship than an ability to speak truthfully with one another. Thus Calvin observed that though God in this commandment may have specifically singled out the term "false witness," suggesting the importance of truthful testimony in a court of law, nevertheless God intended for this doctrine to apply to all calumny, all untrue reports, and all oblique references that tend to defame our neighbors or mar their good reputation. God did so because God wills that we be friends so that no one may be attacked, whether by reputation of the person or in terms of property. "Whoever then discredits his neighbors, whoever slanders [them] in any way whatever, [only] creates war [and] breaks the bond of charity between men" (*Sermons,* 205).

In John 18:37, Christ before Pilate declares that he has come into the world "to bear witness to the truth" (RSV). Truth is a witness and that to which we witness is Christ who is truth. As Christians we lie to the world when we are ashamed to testify to that which Christ has made possible. We believe that in Jesus Christ the whole of God's truth is manifest. Through the Spirit, as we are told in John 8:32, we have been made free and holy. To follow Jesus, to be witnesses to Jesus through the Spirit, we have been sanctified into the truth (John 17:17).

Therefore, in this commandment to speak the truth to one another we have the Christian life summed up as life for the world. Here we see the truth about God and the truth about ourselves as inseparable. We were created to tell one another the truth through the very gift that God gave us to speak and through speaking to share in judgments that make us friends. Calvin noted:

> Now if we want to observe what this text contains, we need to consider a higher principle, that is to consider why God created our tongues and why he gave us speech, the reason being that we might be able to communicate with each other. Now what is the purpose of human communication if it isn't our mutual support and charity? Consequently, then, it is essential for us to learn to bridle our tongues to the extent that the union which God commands us may constantly be nurtured as much as possible. And that is why Saint James employs such vehemence when he speaks of evil reports. He says that the tongue, which is such a little member, or such a small piece of flesh, can start such a fire as to ravage the largest forests in the world. Therefore let us come back to our principle, knowledge that God provided us with a unique gift when he gave us a means of being able to communicate with each other. So on the one hand men's affections may be hidden, but on the other the tongue exists to reveal our hearts. Therefore let us be encouraged to use such a gift and not to soil it with our vices and deplorableness. And seeing that God has given it to us for the purpose of nurturing tender love and fraternity with each other, may we not abuse it in order to gossip and bustle about here and there, so perverting our speech as to poison ourselves against each other. (*Sermons,* 216)

Here we see that it is quite right to think that the Ten Commandments reveal who we are. That is what the church has traditionally maintained by suggesting that law is "natural." We've been created to tell one another the truth. God gave us tongues in order to speak truthfully. Augustine, in his famous treatise "On Lying," says plainly that a "lie consists in speaking falsehood with the intention of deceiving." We owe it to one another as creatures of a good God to tell one another the truth. That requires learning great skill since, confronted with this command, we find ourselves captured by falsehood.

There is no sin more precious to the devil than the lie, for the devil knows that we never lie more readily than when we do so in the name of a love that is undisciplined in the truth of Christ's cross and resurrection. Thus in John 8:44 we learn that the devil is liar and the father of all lies. And from lies we die a deadly death. Therefore as the witnesses to Christ's cross and resurrection we are called to speak the truth and thus disclose the lies that lead to violence and death.

For instance, many doctors and nurses, when asked why they did not tell the truth to a seriously ill patient, justify their lack of candor on the basis of love. "I didn't think the patient really wanted to hear that he was dying."

Such "love" is the source of our lies. Patients are given false hope, hope based not on the truth of Christ's death and resurrection, but hope based upon a lie. The patient is encouraged to live in a dreamworld, is denied the opportunity to put life in order in the face of death, is robbed of the joy that might come, in the last days of life, from reconciliation with family, friends, and God. Lies shaped by such undisciplined and malformed "loves" are among the most deadly. Such lies not only make us liars, but also act as if God lies, for, to tell the truth, God has created us to be the sort of people who can hear the truth about our condition (that we are all "terminal") without despair.

Preachers who do not preach truthfully often justify their pastoral deceit on the basis of "love." They are such kind and caring pastors, they don't want to make their congregations' lives more miserable by telling them the truth. Congregations complain that this makes for boring, predictably trite sermons. What they ought to be complaining about is paternalistic pastors who have so little respect for their congregations as to assume that they are fated to be liars. Moreover, if the church cannot maintain a truthful ministry how can we expect others with public responsibility and offices to learn to say the truth?

Thus Luther argued that lying and law courts are closely associated in this commandment because:

> Where judges, mayors, princes, or others in authority sit in judgment, we always find that, true to the usual course of the world, men are loathe to offend anyone. Indeed, they speak dishonestly with an eye of gaining favor, money, prospects, or friendship. Consequently, a poor man is inevitably oppressed, loses his case, and

suffers punishment. It is the universal misfortune of the world that men of integrity seldom preside in courts of justice.

A judge ought, above all, to be a man of integrity, and not only upright but also a wise, sagacious, brave, and fearless man. Likewise, a witness should be fearless; more than that, he should be an upright man. (*The Large Catechism,* 43-44)

Luther truthfully describes who we are. We have been given tongues to speak the truth to one another so we are capable of friendship with one another and with God. Another name for such friendship is the life of charity. Yet the very means we have been given creates the temptation to lie, to "love" in the wrong way. Here we see how all sins are tied together: We are tempted to lie in the interests of protecting the past lies on which our friendships depend. The very modes we have of protecting ourselves, modes that have much to be said for them, such as civility and politeness, can become ways we lie to one another by refusing to tell one another the truth.

For example, civility is enlisted in our efforts to keep the truth from ourselves. We would rather be polite than truthful. Thus some feminists, in their critique of current calls to civility, are suspicious that those who recommend civility do so in an effort to silence the truth that women have to tell men. They should be suspicious. Who wants to know the truth that when confronted with our lies we must confess that we are sinners and desire not to be what we were created to be?

Calvin noted:

This precept even extends to forbidding us to affect a fawning politeness barbed with bitter taunts under the guise of joking. Some do this who crave praise for their witticisms, to others' shame and grief, because they sometimes grievously wound their brothers with this sort of impudence. Now if we turn our eyes to the Lawgiver, who must in his own right rule our ears and heart no less than our tongue, we shall surely see that eagerness to hear detractions, an unbecoming readiness to make unfavorable judgments, are alike forbidden. For it is absurd to think that God hates the disease of evilspeaking in the tongue, but does not disapprove of evil intent in the heart. (*Institutes,* 412-13)

The law court therefore is but the paradigmatic instance that illumines the difficulty of learning to speak truthfully in all conversation. For nowhere do we lie more readily than in the easy speech of the everyday. Truthfulness requires work; lying is lazy. We lazily accept assumed agreements, i.e., "We must oppose naked aggression wherever it occurs around the world." "We find ourselves in a social order in which we govern ourselves." "I'm not all that rich." "Who cares, so long as no one gets hurt?" "I don't have a racist bone in my body." It becomes therefore part of the peculiar witness of Christians to be a people in a world of mendacity to speak the truth to one another.

The Eighth Commandment in Christian Life

In our *Resident Aliens: Life in the Christian Colony* (pp. 118-19) we told the story of a pastor who presented the idea of a day-care center for children to his church's Christian education committee. After all, what could be more justified as ministry than a day-care center?

Gladys butted in, "Why is the church in the day-care business? How could it be a part of the ministry of the church?"

The young pastor patiently went over his reasons again: use of the building, attracting young families, another source of income, the Baptists down the street already having a day-care center.

"And besides, Gladys," said Henry Smith, "you know that it's getting harder every day to put food on the table. It's become a necessity for both husband and wife to have full-time jobs."

"That's not true," said Gladys. "You know it's not true, Henry. It is not hard for anyone in this church, for anyone in this neighborhood to put food on the table. Now there *are* people in this town for whom food on the table is quite a challenge, but I haven't heard any talk about them. They wouldn't be using this day-care center. They wouldn't have a way to get their children here. This day-care center wouldn't be for them. If we are talking about ministry to their needs, then I'm in favor of the idea. No, what we're talking about is ministry to those for whom it has become harder every day to have two cars, a VCR, a place at the lake, or a motor home. That's why we're all working hard and leaving our children.

I just hate to see the church buy into and encourage that value system. I hate to see the church telling these young couples that somehow their marriage will be better or their family life more fulfilling if they can only get another car, or a VCR, or some other piece of junk. Why doesn't the church be the last place courageous enough to say, That's a lie."

Nowhere could truthfulness be better witnessed today than in the church's preaching ministry. We must desire, we must demand, that we hear the truth preached by those set aside to be ministers of the gospel. Is it any wonder that the world does not believe in our Messiah when our preaching has been turned into lies in the interests of caring, comfort, and false friendship? Preaching lies not so much by what is said explicitly but by what is left unsaid, namely, that Christians betray their non-Christian brothers and sisters by an unwillingness to say that the reason we are all so miserable is because we do not worship the true God truthfully.

The major reason given by preachers for not speaking more truthfully is, "People don't come to church to be upset." (They usually make such a statement only in the presence of fellow pastors.) How do they know? Even anger can be better than boredom. How do preachers know that Jesus made a mistake in calling these people to be his disciples? How do preachers know that baptism is ineffective?

Moreover, the church must be a testimony that the truth is known by people who have learned how to trust one another through sharing goods, committing one another to lifelong fidelity, the practice of nonviolence, who do these things because they know they are creatures of a gracious God who would have them worship him in truth. Calvin observed that "whoever bears false witness against his neighbor kills him [because] he robs him and is guilty of whatever evil proceeds from his lie (*Sermons,* 205). The church, in its unfaithfulness and willingness to accommodate itself to the lies of the world, becomes unrecognizable as something other than the world, becomes unintelligible to the extent that it lives as if our God does not exist. Thus the church condemns the world to death, abandoning it to its self-deceit.

Again, it is crucial that as Christians we learn simplicity of speech and life. Chastity of the tongue is a great virtue. To speak the truth requires that we lead truthful lives. That is why truthfulness is a virtue that requires there be difference in how we live and what we say. Without such a virtue, trust is impossible. Without trust we are simply pulled deeper and deeper into the lie of the world. We become people commanded by the devil and not God's good servants.

Of course to be witnesses to the truth does not mean we will be acclaimed. It is hard to be grateful to those who tell us the truth about ourselves. The world loves the lie. Surely that is why the church has often found that martyrdom is the result of Christians living truthfully. Martyrdom points clearly to our destiny to be friends with God, which is a friendship that defeats death. The word *martyr* means in the Greek, "witness." We are commanded not to be false witnesses. Many martyrs, God's witnesses, do not mean to assault the world by their lives; their main intent is simply to be faithful to Christ. Yet they sometimes find that, in their quiet fidelity, the world must silence, suppress, ridicule, or even kill them. A deceitful world is deeply threatened by even one little life lived truthfully. So those who live chaste lives are called prudish. Those who speak the truth are called arrogant, abrasive. Those who live simply are called irresponsible.

We cannot be free from the lie by simply trying very hard to be truthful. Rather, we need one another to know how to speak the truth simply without using it as a weapon to protect our own self-estimations. Even the truth can be used in service to our self-deceit. Be suspicious when we say, "I'm telling you this for your own good." Of course we know we can say the truth in a manner or in a context in which it is a lie. For example, the Pharisees in the trial of Jesus noted that he said he would destroy the Temple in three days and then raise it again. Jesus certainly said that, but the Pharisees used it as a way to speak falsely. So we learn to be suspicious in those moments when we hear, "I tell you this in love," or "Let me be frank." Learning to speak truthfully and well requires others loving us enough to tell us when we are caught in the lie, even the lie that says it is in service to the truth.

That is the reason Matthew 18 is so important. We cannot simply acquiesce in our lies with one another, but rather we must love one another enough to name the sins that have captured us. Truth telling apart from a truthful community (i.e., church) seems to us an impossibility.

Calvin noted:

> We must not call "black" "white" under the pretext that we are forbidden to offend anyone. And this is readily observed. For there are a number who would especially like to see nothing condemned and who would even approve of disguising the language. [For example], a thief should not be called by another title and crimes should not be condemned under their proper names. We know that. Moreover, when it comes to blaming the guilty parties who have not only offended God but who are responsible for corrupting everything else, who constitute an infection that contaminates everything, if we want to convict them and proceed in a vigorous manner we must, immediately some of these fastidious people will become angry. (*Sermons,* 211-12)

Therefore it becomes particularly important that we know how to name for one another the evils that we do. Without just descriptions we will always enter into the self-deceptive practice of calling the evil we do good. We will call ourselves victims when we fail to tell the truth about our complicity in our pain. We will speak of others as enemies, oppressors when Jesus has commanded us to call them neighbors. Of course, this is how the power of the lie works.

We suspect no sin is more prevalent in our time, and perhaps in all times, than flattery. We want to be friends, and to be friends we learn to tolerate evils in our friends because we fear losing friendship. Thus we become skilled at maintaining superficial friendship through flattery. Again, as Calvin observed:

> Today the world has come to the point that it seems that we are not good friends and are not faithful and loyal to those with whom we associate unless we acquiesce in their favor when they are wrong. When they are guilty and we ought to be calling this to their attention and chastising them, we turn to eloquent perjury instead.... That is how we esteem God's truth. That is how we

change it into a lie. [And] that is how we also abuse this principle of not slandering our neighbors. (*Sermons*, 209-10)

We are not suggesting that Christians should be moral scolds running around exposing to one another our pettiness. But we are suggesting that our pettiness, which may often seem quite inoffensive, can turn out to be the source of our violence to one another. "Eloquent perjury" ultimately does violence to the person it claims to be protecting. That is why if we are to be nonviolent, we must learn to be capable of hearing from one another judgments we do not wish to hear.

That is why we are asked to make peace with one another before making Eucharist to God. With all the truth telling and truth receiving that ought to go on in the congregation, there is always enough conflict and division to need to make peace. Truth, in the church, is not to be determined by majority vote, but rather truth names the unity discovered through reconciliation.

Perhaps nowhere has the church more betrayed the world than in the support American Christians have given to democracy. We tell ourselves that the people rule, and that through the people's rule we are more likely to live in a truthful politic. That is a lie. It is a lie because even if the people ruled, it would not be truthful since we know that "the people" love the lie. Nowhere is the lie more apparent than when we say we believe we are "the greatest nation in the world" because our nation allegedly believes in freedom. But there can be no freedom that does not acknowledge God. The Constitution attempted to construct a government without God, that is, a government "of the people, for the people, and by the people." We thought we had made a government where the astute balancing of the selfish claims of the people (i.e., rights) would add up to some reason for being a nation. A government based upon the premise that people will be selfish and aggressively self-seeking does not disappoint itself. Treat people as self-centered consumers of freedom and they will respond accordingly. Forsaking the Christian conviction that we were created by God to live of, for, and by the truth, we get people who merely live by hoarding stuff.

Here again we see the issue raised concerning authority in the honoring of father and mother. Americans believe the way to avoid the issue of truth in politics is to assume the truth will be found through public consensus. Democracy is an attempt to get around the necessity for a hierarchy of virtue by majority vote. Rule by king is exchanged for rule by the people, who then are assumed to be the king. But that is not the truth. Rather such a polity is too often the tyranny of shared flattery. Any authority that is true is one that derives its authority from the One alone to whom we rightly give our love and loyalties. That One is God. That democratic speech is speech that has become the lie is but an indication that the church has relinquished our political service to the world by underwriting the lies necessary to govern a world that no longer acknowledges God.

For instance, we had real sympathy with President Clinton's short-lived attempt to get us to be honest about our racism. Normally, the role of a president is periodically to tell us how well we are doing as a people in exchange for our telling him how well he is doing by reelecting him to four more years of national flattery. However, it quickly became clear in Clinton's abortive discussion on race that we did not have the resources to admit to our history in black and white, the depth of mistrust and suspicion between races, the way in which we have made race itself a major modifier of American life, a means of entitlement and identity. Lacking a God who forgives, we dare not tell the truth about our past. Bereft of a means of naming ourselves with more interesting signifiers than "white" or "black," we cannot free ourselves from our collective deceit.

Harsh words. And we wish we had some solution. But we do not. There is, however, hope, because we know God is the Lord and, therefore, despair is not an option for the Christian. We know God has not abandoned us to our own devices. Truth prevails. Not the least, truth prevails through beauty. God, as the author of this world, continues to pull us to the truth through its sheer beauty. A cloudless North Carolina day can serve to remind us that we were created for enjoyment and praise of God and that, in order to praise a God of truth as we ought, we must be truthful.

We were created in the image of God, and this truth often finds its best expression through beauty. It may seem odd, in a world that prizes science as the determiner of any truth, that we believe art (and in its activity much science is art) is perhaps the best means we have of discovering the truth about our lives. What could be more challenging for Christians today than to learn to speak eloquently again to one another, an eloquence that has the beauty of simplicity, so that we might be saved from the elaborate, baroque lies that dominate our lives now? Such art is our morality just to the extent that it makes us truthful witnesses to God, and thus through us the world learns the truth about God. Lying can begin in the singing of cheap, sentimental songs in church. On the other hand, a great deal of truthfulness is engendered by a good hymnal. It is good to sing the truth before we say it. A church building that lies about God, in shoddy, fake architectural nostalgia, will tend to produce Christians who lie.

But to go to church on a summer Sunday, to settle down for a pleasant hour with people like us, planning to be soothed by the music of the organ, lulled by the mellifluous words of the preacher—then to be told the truth, and to be told it straight, thereby to discover we are called to truthful witness, is grand.

Chapter Nine

> *You shall not covet your neighbor's house; you shall not covet*
> *your neighbor's wife, or male or female slave, or ox, or donkey, or*
> *anything that belongs to your neighbor.*
>
> — Exodus 20:17

The Ninth & Tenth Commandments

One thing we have enjoyed about the commandments is their direct, basic simplicity, so wonderfully tied to the concrete stuff of everyday life. Here, in these final commandments, it is as if we have moved away from the externals of life into the dark regions of the human heart, that territory where Jesus claimed that most of the really bad things in this world are hatched (Mark 7:25).

The Hebrew word used for "covet" also entails "lust," which is helpful and honest because that is how our enviousness usually feels, as a lustful desire for something that is another's. Some have said that these commands ought only to apply to *actions* that arise out of covetousness. But we cannot be done with these commandments that simply. In making matters of the heart, inclinations and feelings, a concern of the commandments, dealings between us and God have been taken to a deeper, more perplexing level. Here is a God who does not deal in the modern dichotomy between the inner and the outer, the subjective and the objective, the personal and the communal. It is all of one piece. God is concerned with not only what we do, but also how we feel, what we desire—the things of the heart.

Therefore we will treat the ninth and the tenth commandments as one. We are not unique in this, as commentators within the Christian tradition have often done so. We believe they are so combined because fundamentally the ninth and the tenth commandments are about *desire*. So here in the last commandments we discover what the whole Decalogue is about—namely, that we were created to love God, and when that love is misdirected, life degenerates into a jumble of disordered desires, fragments testifying that we were meant to be something quite else than what we have become. No one has named this desire better than Augustine:

> Late have I loved Thee, O Beauty so ancient and so new; late have I loved Thee: for behold Thou wert within me, and I outside; and I sought Thee outside and in my unloveliness fell upon those lovely things that Thou hast made. Thou wert with me, and I was not with Thee. I was kept from Thee by those things, yet had they not been in Thee, they would not have been at all. Thou didst call and cry to me to break open my deafness: and Thou didst send forth Thy beams and shine upon me and chase away my blindness: Thou didst breathe fragrance upon me, and I drew in my breath and do now pant for Thee: I tasted Thee, and now hunger and thirst for Thee: Thou didst touch me, and I have burned for Thy peace.[1]

"You have made us for yourself, O Lord, and our heart is restless until it rests in you." These words of Augustine's *Confessions* are at the heart of the Decalogue. Only God can satisfy our large desire because we are created by God to be loved by God and to love in return. Nothing else can ever satisfy the depth of that longing. There are some religions that appear to have as their goal the extinguishing of desire, the making of people who have so detached themselves that they no longer burn with need. Christianity is not like that. Our problem as humans is not that we are full of desire, aflame with unfulfillment. Our problem is that we long for that which is unfulfilling. We attempt to be content with that which can never satisfy. As C. S. Lewis said, we are far too easily pleased.

The hard question is never, "How can we come to believe in God?" Rather, the question is, "How we can avoid God?" God has made us for communion with our Creator. Everywhere we look, there is God. God is an incessant lover who would have us as his own and has given us every good gift to be such. It takes great cunning on our part to avoid God, for God is, well, *relentless.* Indeed, even in our sins God has made us to testify to God's goodness.

The Law is meant not only as a mirror to reveal our desire of God but also to expose the disordered character of our desires. Calvin put the matter this way:

> Whenever we are not only too negligent, but equally inclined to flatter ourselves in our vices, ... let us hold up this mirror and take a good look at ourselves. Let us not be deceived. A man can be smudged and people laugh at him while he himself will not see a thing, but let him look in a mirror and see how his face is besmeared and he will hide himself; he will wash it off. Now we need to do the same. For in truth the whole law of God is like a mirror which reflects our filth, its purpose being to confound us and make us ashamed of our shamefulness. But we have to come to this commandment in order to have the right mirror.... For if we only read: "You shall not be a thief, You shall not be a murderer, You shall not be an adulterer," then we would each think that we are innocent. But when we come to this commandment: "You shall not covet," then that provides God with a sharper lancet for not only sounding the bottom of our heart, but all our thoughts and imaginations. Everything within us becomes exposed and brought to consciousness; even what we have not considered sin, God must judge and condemn, unless we have done the same before hand. (*Sermons,* 232-33)

In this commandment, as Calvin saw so well, the Law is never just concerned with externalities but with our soul. Another name for soul is desire. With this sharp "lancet," God hereby performs open-heart surgery. Our hearts are revealed, "exposed and brought to consciousness." In the Law God provides us with a perfect and just rule, but when confronted with such a rule, we find we do not desire it. Indeed, some are so clever as to use the

Law as a way to avoid the Law. They think the Law can be obeyed without desire, but God would not have it so. Rather the Law is meant, as Calvin noted, "to purge ourselves of all wicked affections and all corrupt thoughts to the extent that everything within us directs us toward the goal of fully surrendering ourselves to God" (*Sermons,* 225). "Legalism" therefore turns out to be a way of naming the sin of desiring righteousness without righteousness being a gift of God, the fruit of rightly ordered desire. "We imitate whom we adore," said Augustine. The Law is given to make us more adoring, more desirous of God, not by push but by pull.

Aquinas observed that the reason for this commandment is that our desire has no limits because desire itself is boundless (*The Catechetical Instructions,* 11). Our desire is boundless because it is meant to find its rest—that is, its perfect source and object—in God. The classical Christian word for this is *concupiscence,* which does not mean "sensuality," though it has often been interpreted as that—namely, as a disordered desire. Rather, concupiscence names the intensity of our desire, which, when turned away from God, distorts everything we do and do not do. That is why only the pure of heart will see God (Matthew 5:8). Because what could be a greater gift than purity, that is, the desire to wholly love God as God's good creatures?

Desire is contagious. We desire according to the desires of another because all desire is imitative. I want this or that because someone else wants this or that. That we learn desire from one another means that we desperately desire one another's approval, even though our desires put us in envious conflict with one another.

The disordered nature of our desires, a disorder we learn from one another, leads to violence. Nowhere is that better seen than in the everyday, all too ordinary sins of greed and envy. We think we deserve what our neighbor has, and anything our neighbor has that we do not have diminishes us. The socialist calls capitalism "legalized greed," and the capitalist calls socialism "legalized envy," and both have truth in what they say. Social systems based upon schemes for organizing people like us will inevitably be institutionalized resistance to the ninth and tenth commandments.

We think of life as a zero-sum game. Accordingly, we want what our neighbor has and we are led to an endless cycle of acquisition that never satisfies. American consumptive habits fueled by capitalism are but the most obvious form of this behavior. We think our lives will be less if we don't have "the latest," but then we discover that the latest becomes dated almost before we get it home. The rapid development of computers makes them a particularly gruesome master for those who must have the latest.

We live in a world of manufactured need since we no longer have any idea of what we need. Advertising creates desire. We did not know we needed a medicine for heartburn until TV told us. We did not even know heartburn was an affliction. The surest way to drive someone crazy in modernity is to ask the pressing question: *What do you really want?* It turns out that we do not know what we want other than we want it and we want it now.

In the movie *Jaws,* when the huge shark—the animal called a "vast eating machine"—is caught and killed the shark is taken into a marine laboratory and dissected. Out of the stomach of the shark are pulled fish, an old tire, bones, a piece of a boat, and a clock.

A priest friend of ours said that, at that point in the movie, he exclaimed, "That's my congregation!"

We are so very desirous, so deeply empty and hungry, so omnivorous.

In Genesis, after the rebellion and sin of humanity, God tells Adam that, because of his sin, work will now be drudgery, a ceaseless treadmill of struggle with the earth. To the woman, God says that she shall "desire" her husband but that he shall rule over her. Childbearing shall be painful. This is not the state of the world as God intended, for Genesis clearly shows that God created male and female as coworkers in the good garden.

Unfortunately, because of our disordered desire (desire to fulfill hunger even when we have had enough is what brought us to grief with the fruit of the forbidden tree) women and men now live in a state of war. Those who had been given the gift of sex to "be fruitful and multiply" now enlist sex as another weapon in their arsenal. Those who were created to be friends are now enemies, competitors.

Children, the fruit of our desire, become additional possessions. We need to rule over someone. Children continually frus-
trate parents' desire to be their masters. Children's better natures
tell them that their lives are gifts of God rather than part of our
household inventory. So they resist and rebel, and we despise
them for it. We envy our friends whose children "turn out well,"
and in turn our children envy us for not giving them all their
hearts' desire.

The abuse of children and spouses has a common root. Domestic violence is a symptom of family life after the Fall, of people
being married and having children for no better reason than fulfillment of disordered desire. Again, how interconnected are all the
commandments. First we want a new car, then we must have a
new spouse worthy of the new car, then children who tell us that
we are the perfect parents we wish we were, then an obedient dog
to go with the adoring kids and . . . is it any wonder that most murder is committed by those in our own homes? Covetousness leads
to death. All the commandments are connected.

Of course, acquisition of a better house, a better CD player, a
better job, will allow us to acquire even more and is but the
grossest form of vices associated with *greed*. A recent PBS docu-
mentary calls our sickness "affluenza" but we, being suspicious of
the world's new words, prefer greed. It's sin, not sickness. The
problem is that, in the world in which we live, we have learned
to call greed "ambition" or "providing for my family." We have
learned to call greed "getting ahead." We have learned to call
greed "working for a better life." We have learned to call greed
"pleasure." As Calvin might put it, we have managed to blacken
our mirrors so that we no longer see ourselves.

The good thing about greed is that unlike some sin, it is not
subtle. Its results are public, there for all to see. Accumulation
tends toward conspicuous display. If we cannot show others
what we have accumulated, what's the good of accumulation?
Envy, the close cousin of greed, is infinitely more subtle. Envy
loves to adorn itself as "service to others" through which we
acquire power in order to "do some good." We climb to the top
of the company ladder, not for ourselves, but in service to the
advancement of all women everywhere. We become the corpo-

rate attorney so that we can give a few hours a month to pro bono work. We say all we want is simply to be able to do what good we can do. Our want is the root of the problem. Desire. What we want is power and status. Like the rich fool in Jesus' parable, we attempt to resist knowledge of our own insignificance by insulating ourselves with things. Alas, we find that no matter what we have acquired, there is always someone we envy. Our sense of diminishment demands to be fed. Even Solomon despaired when the Queen of Sheba showed him her palace.

The commandment against covetousness may be one of the most accusatory for those of us who live in a society of seemingly unquenchable acquisitiveness, where greed appears to be a necessary component to keep the economy running smoothly. The Constitution tells us that America exists to give people what we want, without judging the comparative worth of our wants. To not want is almost un-American.

A friend of ours had a grandfather who was one of the founders of Woolworth's department store. His grandfather's great contribution, which was to revolutionize merchandising, was the bright idea to put the merchandise out on tables and in showcases for everyone to see. Before that invention, people would enter a store and tell a clerk what they wanted. The clerk would go and obtain for them the merchandise in the storage area and present it to the customer for purchase. His grandfather was the first to lay the merchandise out on the table to be seen and touched and savored. And the rest is history. His invention was perfect for a people who now no longer know how even to name what we want. Show us everything and we shall invent a desire for it all.

The Ninth and Tenth Commandments in Christian Life

In our world today we are constantly bombarded with stimuli to our covetousness. As we said when we discussed the prohibition against killing, we cannot depend on our own will to be faithful to the demands of the commandments in such a society. We need a community, the church, to enable us to rise above our natural covetousness and the rather relentless formation into greediness that characterizes this economy.

When you take a child into Toys R Us you do not have to tell the child what to do. That child has, even at a very early age, received relentless training in greed. But if you expect that child to be able to say No! to the lures of this world; if that child is ever to be able to stand up and say, "Enough is enough!" then that child must be formed and re-formed by a people who have learned to want the right things rightly. Again, we call such a people "church."

We believe that the church could do a better job of enabling ordinary Christians to be faithful, that is, to want the right things rightly. We expect that we American Christians must gain better skills in analysis, discernment, and resistance if we are to have lives that are congruent with the demands of the commandments. In Will's last congregation, we had a young couples' church school class that selected for study a curriculum then offered by our denomination called "TV and Christian Values." The course involved such tasks as analyzing television advertisements, keeping a log of family viewing habits, discerning the hidden messages behind programs. The course seemed to us a waste of time.

To show how little we knew, the class doubled in size in two months.

These young couples knew. It is not only the "idiot box." It is the "ideology box." TV is about indoctrination, inculcation into an ideology alien to our theology. And it's winning.

We predict the church of the future will take seriously the task of equipping the saints, of giving people the skills they need to resist, to see the church and its educational ministry as a means of remedy for sin, training in subversion, detoxification.

There is no way to will our way out of disordered desire. The Law helps us to discover our sin, but, as Paul noted, the Law itself cannot of itself save us. Salvation requires the ordering of our desires through friendships made possible by God's good desires made manifest in Cross and Resurrection. In such friendship we begin to taste what perfect friendship with God entails. Thus we are lured, enticed toward perfect communion with God. Augustine, for whom conversion turned lust into desire, described it this way:

There will true glory be, when no one will be praised by mistake or flattery; true honor will not be refused to the worthy, nor granted to the unworthy; likewise, no one unworthy will pretend to be worthy, where only those who are worthy will be admitted. There true peace will reign, where no one will experience opposition either from self or others. God Himself will be virtue's reward; He gives virtue and has promised to give himself as the best and greatest reward that could exist. "I shall be their God and they will be my people." This is the meaning of the Apostle's words: "So that God may be all in all." God Himself will be the goal of our desires; we shall contemplate Him without end, love Him without surfeit, praise Him without weariness. This gift, this state, this act, like eternal life itself, will assuredly be common to all. (*City of God*, 22-23)

The Communion of Saints names a community in which there is no zero-sum game. Rather, each person's gifts build up the whole community. We believe that through the Holy Spirit we have been made part of that communion now. Sunday is dress rehearsal for eternity. Nowhere is such communion more deeply embodied than when we share the body and blood of Christ in the Eucharist, thus becoming God's good sacrifice to the world. In that sacrifice God brings to an end the necessity of our victimizing one another in the interests of bringing some end to the disorder of our desires.

In an immortal poem, John Donne speaks of that eucharistic transformation when we have been found by God, and our heart is ravished, battered by the onslaught of a loving God:

> *Batter my heart, three person'd God; for You*
> *As yet but knocke, breathe, shine, and seeke to mend:*
> *That I may rise, and stand, o'erthrow mee, 'and bend*
> *Your force, to breake, blowe, burn and make me new.*
> *I, like an usurpt towne, to'another due,*
> *Labour to'admit You, but Oh, to no end,*
> *Reason Your viceroy in mee, mee should defend,*
> *But is captiv'd, and proves weake or untrue.*
> *Yet dearly "I love You," and would be loved faine,*
> *But am betroth'd unto your enemie:*
> *Divorce mee, untie, or breake that knot againe,*
> *Take mee to You, imprison mee, for I*

Except You' enthrall mee, never shall be free.
Nor ever chast, except You ravish mee.[2]

For us, one of the most relevant moments in the Sunday service is when, as we come forward for the Eucharist, the church tells us to hold out our hands to receive. There, before the altar, with empty hands outstretched, we are empty, open, receptive, hungry. The church has reformed us from those who seize and grab and clutch into those who graciously receive. Our desire has been reformed, our lives bent toward the God who promised blessing for the hungry.

In the Eucharist we find the full reality of the Law, for there we discover that God has not abandoned us. In the Eucharist the Law is given its *telos,* creating peace in a world that knows no peace. Our hungers are named not as longing for the stuff of this world, but by a bit of bread and a sip of wine we learn to call just this much bread and this much wine a feast. It is all the more important therefore, for Christians to have our desires ordered by this great feast through which we learn God's love as truly unrelenting, seeking us all the way to the Cross.

In this feast of victory, we are given our hearts' desire, even before we know how to name what we desired. We are fed, miraculously to discover that a bit of bread, a sip of wine, has satisfied our hunger. We then know that the psalmists were not indulging in mere hyperbole when they sang,

Oh, how I love your law!
It is my meditation all day long.
Your commandment makes me wiser than my enemies,
for it is always with me.
I have more understanding than all my teachers, . . .
How sweet are your words to my taste,
sweeter than honey to my mouth!

—Psalm 119:97-99, 103

Notes

1. Augustine, in *The Oxford Book of Prayer,* ed. George Appleton (Oxford, N.Y.: Oxford University Press, 1985), 65.

2. John Donne, in Carl Hermann Voss, *The Universal God: An Interfaith Anthology of Man's Eternal Search for God* (Cleveland and New York: Word Publishing Co., 1953).

Bibliography

Aquinas, Thomas. *The Catechetical Instructions of St. Thomas Aquinas.* Translated by Rev. Joseph B. Collins. New York: Joseph Wagner, 1939.

Augustine. *The City of God.* Translated by Henry Bettenson. New York: Penguin Books, 1972.

Barth, Karl. *Church Dogmatics,* 3/4. Translated by A. T. Mackay et al. Edinburgh: T & T Clark, 1961.

Calvin, John. *Institutes of the Christian Religion.* Translated by Ford Lewis Battles. Philadelphia: The Westminster Press, 1960.

Calvin, John. *John Calvin's Sermons on the Ten Commandments.* Translated by Benjamin Farley. Grand Rapids, Mich.: Baker Book House, 1980.

Catechism of the Catholic Church. Liguori, Mo.: Liguori Publication, 1994.

Heschel, Abraham Joshua. *The Sabbath.* New York: Farrar, Straus, and Giroux, 1951.

Luther, Martin. *The Large Catechism.* Translated by Robert Fischer. Philadelphia: Fortress Press, 1959.

McCabe, Herbert. *What Ethics Is All About.* Washington: Corpus Books, 1969.

Wesley, John. *Explanatory Notes on the Old Testament.* Salem, Oh.: Schmul Publishing, 1975.

Index

Biblical Index